D1260557

THE FLORIDA KEYS
VOLUME 3

The Wreckers

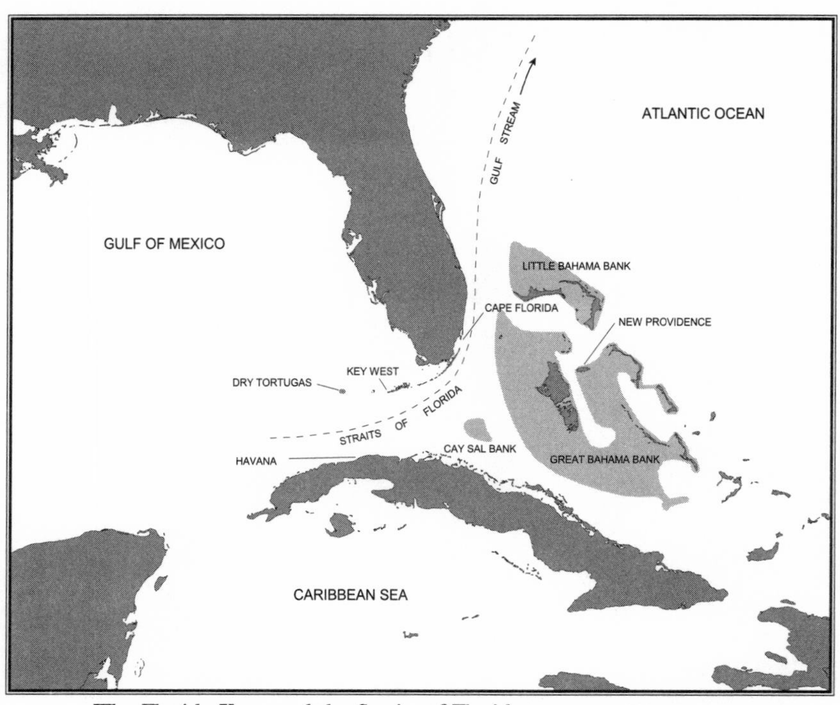

The Florida Keys and the Straits of Florida (drawing by Erich Mueller)

THE FLORIDA KEYS

VOLUME 3

The Wreckers

John Viele

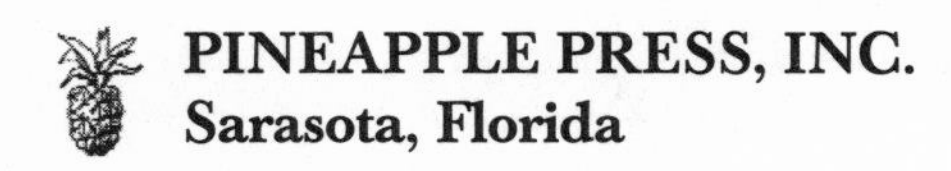

To Gail Swanson, Tom Hambright, and my wife, Pam,
who have been of such great help to me

Inquiries should be addressed to:

Pineapple Press, Inc.
P.O. Box 3889
Sarasota, Florida 34230

www.pineapplepress.com

Library of Congress Cataloging-in-Publication Data

Viele, John. 1923–
The Florida keys volume 3 : the wreckers / John Viele. —1st ed.
p. cm. — (Florida's history through its places)
Includes bibliographical references and index.
ISBN 1-56164-219-3 (alk. paper)
1.Florida Keys (Fla.)—History. 2. Florida Keys (Fla.)—Social life and customs. 3. Florida Keys (Fla).—Biography. I. Title. II. Series.

F317.M7V54 1996
975.9'41—dc20

95-50036

First Edition
10 9 8 7 6 5 4 3 2

Design by Carol Tornatore
Composition by Shé Heaton
Printed in the United States of America

"First came the wreckers . . . to prey upon the carcasses of dead ships; then came the merchants and traders to prey upon the wreckers; then came the doctors and lawyers to prey upon both the traders and the wreckers; and last came the clergy of all denominations to pray for all."

–One commentator in 1851

Contents

Acknowledgments

I am indebted to the many historians and writers who have researched wreck salvaging in the Florida Keys before me and made their work available to the public in scholarly studies, books, and articles. Of those I know, I would particularly like to thank the following: Tom Hambright, director of the Florida History Department, Monroe County Public Library for preparing a detailed index of the nearly one thousand cases in the Admiralty Final Record Books of the federal court at Key West, for sharing his comprehensive, detailed knowledge of Keys history with me, and for leading me to many sources I would not otherwise have discovered; Gail Swanson, Keys historian, for her thorough research of the story of the wreck of the slave ship *Guerrero*, which she made available to the Monroe County Public Libraries; Dr. Eugene Lyon, former director of the Center for Historic Research at Flagler College, Saint Augustine, and recognized authority on the sixteenth-century Spanish presence in Florida, for sharing his knowledge of Spanish salvage expeditions to the Keys with me; Jack Haskins, treasure salvor, diver, and researcher, for his translations of Spanish archival documents and answers to my questions on the 1733 Spanish salvage operations; David Whall, retired naval officer and salvage diver, for providing me with the results of his research into wrecks on the Florida Reef; and Jim Clupper, Keys historian and manager of the Monroe County Public Library, Islamorada, for making available the many sources of Keys history he has discovered.

Molly Wylly, former director of the Audubon House Museum, originally the home of wrecking captain John H. Geiger, was most helpful in providing me with the results of her research into the life of Captain Geiger and in reviewing my story of his wrecking career, for which I am deeply appreciative.

My thanks also go to Eugene Lytton, former mayor of Monroe County, and his wife, Catherine Lytton, for furnishing me with genealogical data and other information they have uncovered on the life of Catherine's great-grandfather, wrecking captain Richard Roberts.

I was fortunate to be able to find several talented artists to help illustrate the book. James Lloyd, a retired design engineer, contributed drawings of a Spanish diving bell and a Keys lighthship. Wayne Giordano sketched a drawing of wreckers working in a cargo hold, and Lamar Ball called on his imagination to produce a scene of Keys natives attacking the crew of a shipwrecked Spanish galleon.

Once again, I am particularly indebted to Claudia Jew, assistant manager of photographic services at the Mariners' Museum, for her helpfulness and high-quality work in fulfilling my order for archival photographs, all while she was recovering from a serious illness. I thank Joan Morris, director of the photographic collections at the Florida State Archives, and Adolph Gucinski, contract photographer for the Monroe County Public Library, who delivered fine photographic reproductions of historic images in a timely manner. I am grateful to Nancy Jameson, former director of the Oldest House and Wreckers Museum at Key West, who gave me useful inputs from her research into wrecking captains and granted me permission to reproduce the museum's poster, "Wreck Ashore!," drawn by Kathleen Elgin.

I would like to express my sincere thanks for the help I received from all the staff of the Monroe County Public Library at Key West, in particular Mary Ann Duchardt of the Reference Department and Lynda Hambright of the Florida History Department.

I am most grateful to Dr. Erich Mueller, director of the Mote Marine Laboratory, Center for Tropical Research at Summerland Key, Florida, for donating his valuable time and graphic arts skills to produce the maps of the Florida Keys and Florida Reef.

Finally, I should not forget to thank my wife, Pam, for the countless hours she spent at the computer entering and compiling wrecking data. Even though I did not always express it, I am sincerely appreciative of her honest and helpful appraisals of my writing.

Introduction

This book, the third in a series on the history of the Florida Keys, is about the wreckers of the Florida Keys, the daring seamen who sailed out in fair weather or foul and risked their lives and vessels to save men, ships, and cargoes cast up on the Florida Reef.

Stories of wreckers have long captured the interest and imagination of the public. Books like *Reap the Wild Wind*, which was made into a movie starring John Wayne, short stories like John Hersey's "God's Hint" about the preacher who was also a wrecker, magazine articles, and newspaper accounts have portrayed wreckers in many roles from swashbuckling heroes to ruthless pirates. Unfortunately, most of these tales have showed the wreckers in an unfavorable light. Interest in wreckers continues today. Visitors to Key West can see reenactments of wrecking days at the Shipwreck Historeum and tour the homes of prominent wrecking captains at the Oldest House and the Audubon House. Once a year, they can recapture some of the excitement of the cry "Wreck ashore!" when they view the start of the annual Wreckers' Cup Race.

But what was the true character of the wreckers? Were they rogues or saviors? Were they unscrupulous men who thought only of the profit to be made through the misfortunes of others, or were they honest men who performed a humanitarian and vital service to men, ships, and property in distress? This book attempts to answer those questions through true stories of the lives of wrecking captains and factual accounts of salvage operations.

Fronted by a treacherous coral reef, the Florida Keys lie in a 150-mile-long semicircle along the northern and western edges of the Straits of Florida. In the age of sail, the Straits became the favored passage for shipping traffic between ports in the western Caribbean and the Gulf of Mexico and ports along the Atlantic east coast and in Europe. Because of the swift-flowing Gulf Stream current, unpredictable countercurrents, calms in summer, hurricanes in fall, gales in winter, and inaccurate charts, the passage through the Straits was considered one of the most dangerous of any along the American coast. As shipping traffic through the Straits gradually increased, so did the number of shipwrecks. By the 1850s, ships were piling up on the reef at the rate of nearly one a week. It was this harvest of wrecks that gave rise to the wrecking industry, which in turn led to the settlement of Key West and fueled its growth to become, at one time, the most populous and prosperous city in Florida

The story of wrecking starts with the Keys natives, who, beginning in the early 1500s, paddled out to the reef to investigate and plunder shipwrecks. If there were any survivors, the natives usually killed or enslaved them. The next wreckers to arrive in the Keys were the members of Spanish expeditions who came to recover treasure from sunken galleons. Among them were African slaves and Keys natives whom the Spanish employed as salvage divers. The Spanish were followed closely by the Bahamian "wrackers," as they called themselves, who came to hunt turtles and cut hardwood timber as well as to salvage wrecks. They operated in the Keys for nearly one hundred years before the Americans took possession and forced them to leave.

The story of the American wreckers begins after the end of the War of 1812, when New England fishermen began coming to the Keys to fish for the Havana market. They soon discovered the profits to be made from salvaging wrecks and stayed to become early settlers. The story continues through the establishment of Key West as a wrecking center in 1822, the rise and fall of rival wrecking stations, the regulation of wrecking under a federal court with admiralty jurisdiction, the rapid growth of the industry through the wrecking heyday of the 1840s and '50s, the gradual decline in wrecks after the Civil War, and the final days of the sailing wreckers at the beginning of the twentieth century.

Wrecking as practiced in the Florida Keys differed in a number of important respects from wrecking as pursued along other sections of the American coast. For example, the Florida Keys were the only place where wrecking captains and wrecking vessels had to be licensed by a judge of the federal court, who also had the power to revoke those licenses for wrongdoing. On other coasts, salvage vessels normally remained in port until they received a report of a shipwreck. In the Keys, wrecking vessels stationed themselves where the incidence of wrecks was the highest and conducted

Wrecking schooners in a squall racing to a wreck (*The Century Illustrated Monthly Magazine*, Vol. XXIII, Nov. 1881 to Apr. 1882, p. 187. From the collections of The Mariners' Museum, Newport News, Virginia)

searches for wrecks along the reef on a daily basis. And only in the Keys did wreckers have to cope with oppressive heat, hordes of mosquitoes, hostile natives, and angry Spanish slavers.

A primary goal of the research for this book was to learn the truth about how wrecking was conducted in the Florida Keys. Did the wreckers place false lights along the shore to lure ships to their destruction on the reef? Was a mad dash to the waterfront when wrecking crewmen heard the cry "Wreck ashore!" really a common scene in Key West? How did wrecking captains find wrecks so soon after they went ashore, even at night? How did small sailing vessels with crews of just a dozen men, using nothing more than the power of the wind and their muscles, manage to refloat ships one hundred times their size? How were salvage awards determined and who profited most from the business? What was the "Blacklist," and how did certain wrecking captains and crewmen get their names on it?

The principal source for answers to these questions was the Admiralty Final Record Books of the U.S. Superior Court, and later, District Court at Key West, also known as the "wrecking court." These records contain the testimony of wrecking captains and masters of wrecked ships, as well as the opinions and decrees of the judges, for salvage claims from 1829 to 1911. The handwritten records of court cases for 640 wrecks involving more than a thousand wrecking vessels were transcribed from microfilm, studied, and analyzed. Another original source was the diary of a Key West attorney who practiced in the wrecking court during the period 1830 to 1857. His diary contains many comments on decisions of the court, wrecking vessels, and wrecked ships. Contemporary newspapers and documents in the Florida Territorial Papers were also consulted. The Bahamian newspapers from 1784 to 1825, preserved on microfilm, revealed never-before-told tales of Bahamian wreckers' salvage operations and encounters with pirates and privateers while on the Florida Reef.

Because of its strategic position at the entrance to the Gulf of Mexico and gateway to the western Caribbean astride a major shipping lane, Key West soon became an important seaport and naval base, as well as a wrecking center. As background for the wreckers' operations, the book includes the story of the rise of Key West as a seaport. Efforts to make the passage through the Straits of Florida safer by erecting lighthouses and conducting surveys to develop accurate charts are also related, along with their impact on the wrecking industry.

As more and more lighthouses marked the reef (much to the disgust of the wreckers), as accurate charts of the Keys and the reef became available, and as steam replaced sail, the days of the sailing wreckers drew to an end. In 1921, the federal court closed its register of wrecking licenses, and a hazardous, highly competitive, sometimes lucrative, and often misunderstood way of life passed into history.

Note: The terms "captain" and "master," when used in reference to the person commanding a vessel other than a naval vessel, are nearly synonymous and often used interchangeably. To avoid confusion, in this book I have used "captain" to refer to captains of wrecking vessels and "master" to refer to captains of wrecked vessels.

THE FLORIDA KEYS
VOLUME 3

The Wreckers

Chapter 1

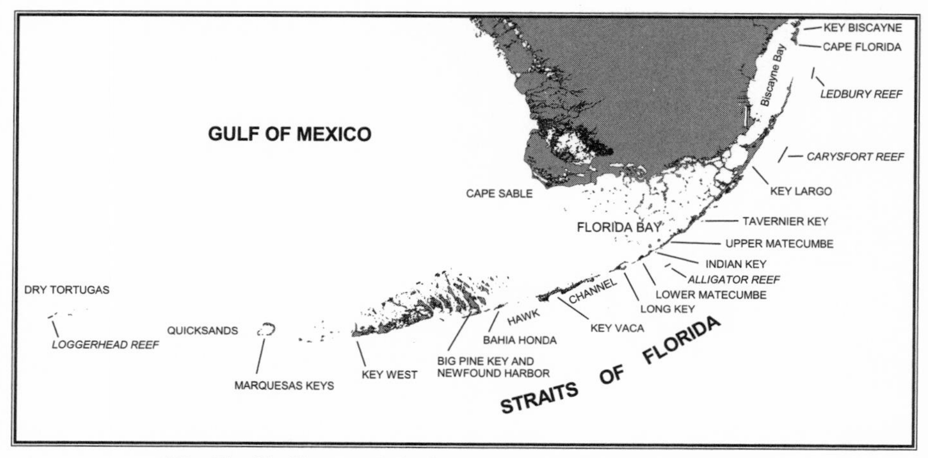

The Florida Keys and the Florida Reef (drawing by Erich Mueller)

PRE-SETTLEMENT WRECKING

The First Wreckers

When the first Spanish galleons sailed through the Straits of Florida carrying treasure from the New World back to Spain, the Keys were inhabited by natives who had lived there for thousands of years. Archaeologists estimate their population as between five hundred and a thousand natives. According to Hernando d'Escalante Fontaneda, a thirteen-year-old boy shipwrecked in the Keys in 1549 and taken captive by the natives, the two main villages were Cuchiaga, located in the lower Keys, and Guarugumbe, situated in the upper Keys, possibly on one of the Matecumbe Keys. Later Spanish documents mention a Chief of the Key of Bones (Key West), a Chief of the Matecumbeses, and the tribal names Cuchiagaros (lower Keys), Bayahondos (Bahia Honda Key area), and Viscaynos (Biscayne Bay area).

The Keys natives were hunter-gatherers. They subsisted principally on fish, sea mammals, turtles, and shellfish but also hunted deer and racoon and gathered wild berries and fruits. They fashioned most of their weapons, tools, and implements from seashells and fishbones and were said to be great archers and spear throwers. Skilled and daring mariners, they made long coastal voyages in dugout canoes and, by the end of the seventeenth century, were crossing the Straits of Florida in large dugouts, presumably rigged with sails, to trade with the Spanish at Havana.

When a Spanish ship piled up on the reef, the natives would paddle out to investigate. If there were any survivors, they usually killed them or enslaved them. Gradually, through contacts with fishermen from Cuba, they grew less hostile to the Spanish but remained a threat to other castaways. Fontaneda's narrative of his experiences as a captive of the Keys natives indicates that they were experienced shipwreck plunderers by the middle of the sixteenth century. He wrote that the natives of the Keys were "rich; but, in the way that I have stated, from the sea [wrecks], not from the land." When English privateer ships under Christopher Newport stopped in

Keys natives would paddle out to a wreck to investigate and plunder. If there were any survivors, they usually killed or enslaved them. (drawing by Lamar Ball)

the Keys to look for water in 1592, the natives of Matecumbe traded gold and silver items they had taken from shipwrecks for sailors' rusty knives. A French priest, shipwrecked in the Keys in 1722, concluded that the only reason the natives stayed on the barren key he landed on was to plunder shipwrecks. Dr. Eugene Lyon, an authority on the sixteenth-century Spanish presence in Florida, expressed it this way: "It also appears that over time they [the Keys natives] adapted to another kind of sea resource–European shipwrecks–and developed the skills of salvaging materials from those wrecks and utilizing them to make items for personal use and adornment."

The Spanish Salvagers

The next shipwreck salvagers to appear on the Keys scene were the Spanish. They came to salvage the wrecks of their treasure-laden galleons. The loss of even one treasure galleon was so critical to Spain's economy that Spanish-American authorities established permanent salvage teams at the principal Caribbean ports of Cartagena, Panama, Vera Cruz, and Havana. Each team consisted of fully equipped salvage vessels and trained salvage divers. At first, the Spanish used native divers of the Caribbean, the best of whom were the native Indians of the Bahamas. But, by the mid 1500s, most of them were gone, victims of European diseases and overwork. Next, they tried using African slaves and found that with training they made excellent divers. They also learned that the natives of the Keys were good divers and, beginning in the early 1600s, used them in a number of salvage operations.

Two major Spanish salvage expeditions to the Keys, one in 1622 and the other in 1733, came about as a result of hurricane disasters to Spanish treasure flotas (fleets). In both instances, the flotas had departed Havana and were in the Straits of Florida on their way back to Spain when the storms struck. As will be seen, the efforts to salvage these ships and their cargoes involved many vessels and divers working over a period of years.

On September 6, 1622, a hurricane struck a flota of twenty-eight ships one day after the ships had left Havana on their return voyage to Spain. The storm drove six of the ships, including three treasure-carrying galleons, onto the reef or into shallow water along the Keys, where they sank either partially or totally. Five hundred fifty passengers and crewmen lost their lives.

The first group of survivors reached Havana ten days after the storm. The governor immediately dispatched a five-vessel salvage expedition to the Keys. With guidance from a survivor, the expedition leader, Gaspar de Vargas, located one of the sunken galleons by the sight of its mizenmast still showing above the water. It was the *Nuestra Señora de Atocha,* sunk in fifty-five feet of water several miles to the west of the Marquesas Keys. Divers reached the galleon's deck and recovered two guns but were unable to gain access to the cargo hold because the hatches had been tightly secured for the storm. Vargas buoyed the wreck with a spare yardarm so that he could find it again should the mast break off. He then searched the area for the galleon *Santa Margarita,* reported to have gone down nearby, but there was no sign of her.

Realizing he would need more equipment and explosives before he could recover anything from the *Atocha,* Vargas sailed westward to the Dry Tortugas, where the third treasure galleon, the *Nuestra Señora Rosario,* was reported to be wrecked. He found the survivors, half-dead from starvation, thirst, and exposure, on one of the larger keys. On another key nearby, he found the crew of a wrecked *patache* (small fast-sailing vessel used to carry dispatches). Despite the wretched condition of the crews, Vargas considered his first duty to recover the treasure from the *Rosario.* Part of the wrecked galleon was still above the surface. To make it easier for his divers to gain access to the cargo hold, Vargas had them set fire to the wreck. After it had burned to the waterline, the divers recovered all of her cargo of silver, worth half a million pesos, as well as some copper and the guns. During the salvage operations, another fierce storm struck the Keys. The rising sea almost completely submerged the island on which the men sought refuge.

Vargas carried the survivors and treasure back to Havana and loaded more supplies and salvage gear to return to the *Atocha.* In the meantime, another salvage expedition sent to search for the missing galleons reported that they were unable to find the *Atocha's* mast, the buoy, or any sign of the *Santa Margarita.* The second storm had torn the hull of the *Atocha* apart and scattered the wreckage over a wide area.

When Vargas returned to the Keys in January the following year, there was no sign of either sunken galleon. He set up a camp on the southwesternmost key of the Marquesas group and began a search for the *Atocha.*

Spanish salvagers dragging for a wreck with chain suspended between two vessels
(Description of Seven Salvage Techniques by Pedro de Ledesma, ca. 1623.
Madrid, *Museo Naval MS. 1035, Seccion C*)

Rowers in launches towed grapnels back and forth over the area while pairs of larger vessels towed long lengths of chain or hemp lines weighted with cannon balls and stones suspended between them. Whenever the grapnels, chains, or weighted lines snagged something on the bottom, divers went down to investigate. The divers from Havana had difficulty reaching the bottom in fifty to sixty feet of water, and some of them became ill. Aware that the black slave divers working the pearl beds around the island of Margarita off the coast of Venezuela could dive deeper, Vargas requested that some of them be sent up to the Keys to help with the search.

Soon Vargas had twenty divers working for him. The dragging and diving continued through the spring and into the summer with little success. The divers found some of the wreckage and recovered two silver bars, but as time wore on, sand piled up over the wreckage, eventually reaching a depth of ten feet. Having lost all hope of finding either the *Atocha* or the *Santa Margarita,* the expedition returned to Havana in August. Before leaving, an engineer made a map of the area and marked the probable site of the *Atocha* with buoys.

Artist's concept of Spanish diving bell with glass ports used to locate the wreck of the *Santa Margarita* (drawing by James Lloyd)

Two years passed before the Spanish salvors returned to the Marquesas Keys. In the meantime, an enterprising politician of Havana, Francisco Nuñez Melián, had obtained a royal contract to allow him to salvage treasure from the galleons. Under the terms of the contract, Melián was to receive one-third of any treasure found, the King would receive one-third, and Melián's expenses would be paid out of the remaining third. In preparation for the work, Melián developed a design for a diving bell with glass viewing ports. Cast in bronze in Havana, the bell weighed 680 pounds. Melián wrote the King of Spain that his diving bell would allow the diver inside "to see the most hidden things," and, as subsequent events proved, he was right.

Melián's expedition arrived in the Marquesas Keys in May 1626 and began towing the bell near the bottom in the area shown on the map made by the previous expedition. Melián promised the slave divers that whoever found one of the galleons would be given his freedom. One day, a slave diver in the bell signaled by tugging on a line that he was leaving the bell to investigate something he had seen. Moments later, the diver broke the surface shouting that he had found the *Margarita.* He went down again and fastened a line to a silver bar. The markings on the bar proved that he had indeed found the *Margarita,* and he was rewarded with his freedom. The water depth at the wreck was thirty feet, well within the capabilities of all the divers. Melián went back to Havana to get more salvage vessels and divers. With thirteen divers working, the expedition recovered 312 bars of silver, silver coins worth 64,000 pesos, a quantity of silverware, the galleon's

Spanish salvage divers working on a submerged wreck (Description of Seven Salvage Techniques by Pedro de Ledesma, ca. 1623. Madrid, *Museo Naval MS. 1035, Seccion C*)

guns, and part of her cargo of copper. At the same time, the search for the *Atocha* continued without success. In August, Melián returned to Havana so that the recovered treasure could be loaded aboard the galleons about to sail for Spain. Another expedition, which included some Guayquiri Indian pearl divers from the island of Margarita, worked the site from November 1626 to January 1627.

During the salvage operations, Keys natives would come to watch in their dugout canoes. Concerned that they might interfere with the operations or destroy the buoys used to mark the wrecks, the Spanish gave them gifts of food and drink. But when another salvage expedition returned in early 1627, they found the natives had burned their camp and supplies. Aware that the natives were accomplished divers and hoping to gain their cooperation, the expeditions' divers taught nine of them how to work as salvage divers and rewarded them with gifts of *melado* (sugar cane syrup), knives, and hatchets.

Beginning in 1627, the Dutch, once more at war with Spain, began harassing the salvage expeditions. That summer, they captured a Spanish longboat sent to check on the buoys marking the *Margarita.* The Dutch turned the twelve crewmembers over to the natives. A *fregata* sent by the governor of Havana to rescue them found them on one of the lower Keys and ransomed them for six jugs of *melado*, twelve hatchets, and six bundles of knives.

The 1627 diving season was a disappointing one for the salvors. Dragging for the *Atocha* resumed while the divers returned to the wreck of the *Margarita.* They had managed to find only four silver bars and a few hundred coins when a Dutch privateer appeared on the scene. As soon as the Spanish got their divers back aboard, they cut their anchor lines and fled back to Havana.

After another season with little treasure recovered and more Dutch raids, Melián gave up active leadership of the salvage work to take up his new duties as governor of Venezuela. He appointed Capt. Juan de Añunez of Havana to carry on the salvage effort, but Añunez had little success.

Fourteen years later, in 1643, Melián received news that Keys natives might have found the *Atocha.* He organized one last salvage expedition to the Marquesas, but the richest galleon of the 1622 flota continued to elude discovery. After a twenty-one-year effort, the search for the *Atocha* was abandoned, and one year later Melián died. One last Spanish attempt to find the *Atocha* was made in 1678. An influential family in St. Augustine obtained permission to make a search. The expedition went to the Marquesas and employed Keys natives as divers. While chasing a sounding turtle, one of the divers sighted a ballast pile, but it was not the treasure galleon. A little over three hundred years passed before a determined American salvor, Mel Fisher, after a sixteen-year search, finally found the *Atocha.*

The next major Spanish salvage operation in the Keys, even larger than the 1622 operation, was the recovery of treasure and other cargo from the ships of the New Spain flota driven ashore in the Keys by the hurricane of July 15–16, 1733. Of the twenty-two ships in the flota, the storm drove nineteen of them ashore along the Keys from Key Vaca to Key Biscayne. Three were treasure-carrying galleons. Because most of the ships were driven over the reef into relatively shallow water, only one of them sank completely, and, considering that the number of crewmen and passengers probably exceeded a thousand, relatively few lives were lost.

When the storm subsided, the battered passengers and crewmen made their way ashore in boats and on rafts. They salvaged what provisions and water they could from the wrecks and built crude shelters from palmetto fronds and wreckage that had drifted onto the beach. There were not nearly enough salvaged provisions to feed everyone, but a far more serious problem was the lack of fresh water.

A passing vessel sighted the wrecked ships and brought news of the disaster to Havana five days after the storm. Within twenty-four hours, nine vessels loaded with food, water, and salvage equipment sailed for the Keys. Also on board were forty salvage divers, a shipbuilder who was experienced in salvage work, and a company of soldiers to guard the recovered treasure.

The castaways gathered in camps near the site of their wrecked ships. The commander of the flota, although his flagship had grounded off Key Largo, established his headquarters on Upper Matecumbe Key because there was a source of fresh water there. The second-in-command, having gone aground off Long Key, set up camp on that key. Other survivors camped on Indian Key and Key Vaca. One can only imagine their misery. In the middle of summer in the Keys, the heat was intense, the sun burned their exposed flesh during the day, and hordes of voracious mosquitoes descended on them in the evening. What little food had been recovered, most of it barrels of raw flour saved from a sloop that did not sink, was served out in tiny rations. The brackish water they found in sinkholes did little to allay their burning thirst. As an official report later noted, "from the voices that break forth in the rising number of people that comprise the camps of the ships, there was no other than water, water, water!"

Despite the miserable condition of the crewmen, their commanders did not delay putting them to work salvaging treasure. Just four days after the storm, they ordered them to return to their ships and begin offloading boxes of silver that were accessible. Ten days after the storm, the salvage divers from Havana arrived, set up camps on the keys adjacent to the wrecks, and began getting out silver from the flooded cargo holds. To facilitate their work, the commanders authorized the salvors to set fire to any ships that could not be refloated.

The overall commander of the flota, General Don Rodrigo de Torres, was especially concerned about the possibility that pirates or wreckers from the Bahamas would discover the wrecked ships and plunder them or even attack the camps where the recovered treasure was stored awaiting shipment back to Havana. He sent an urgent request to Havana to send guns and ammunition and directed the seamen and soldiers to construct two forts, each mounting four small cannons, to protect the treasure at the main camp. He ordered an armed boat to conduct patrols and carry messages along the line of wrecked ships and an armed sloop to stand by the treasure galleons. A ten-gun brigantine escorted the vessels carrying recovered treasure to Havana.

Another of de Torres' concerns was that the divers and others involved in recovering treasure might pilfer some of the silver. He placed guards aboard the ships, on the boats, and on shore to prevent the possibility. But he was still worried that divers working together over an extended period of time might concoct a scheme to secrete some silver and later recover it. To forestall this, he ordered that the divers be rotated between teams and ships.

By August 4, all the treasure on board the *Almiranta* (vice flagship), 1,525 boxes of silver, had been recovered and brought ashore. In two days, divers recovered 180 boxes of silver from the *Infante,* sunk to her decks. By

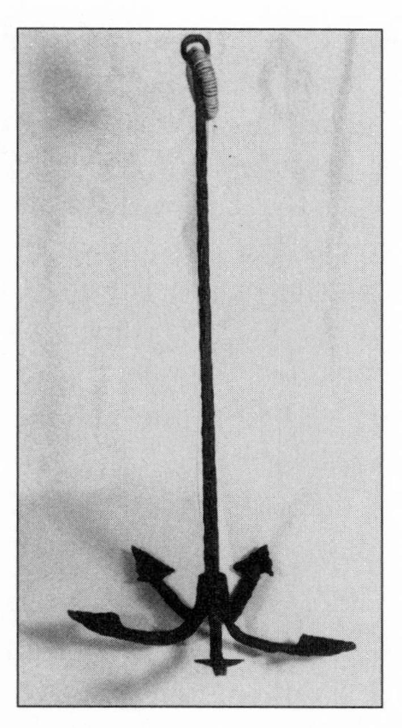

Grapnel used by Spanish salvors to locate submerged wrecks. Recovered from the site of the wreck of treasure galleon *Santa Margarita,* lost in the 1622 hurricane, it was found by Mel Fisher treasure salvor divers in 1999. (courtesy of Mel Fisher Maritime Heritage Society)

August 10, 1,900 boxes of silver had been recovered from the totally flooded *Capitana* (flagship), leaving only 30 not found.

Once they had salvaged the silver, the divers went to work on other cargo, principally cochineal, indigo, and copper. By September, they had brought up 550 copper ingots out of 592 on the *Capitana* and 438 out of 517 on the *Almiranta.* Leakage from the leather bags containing the cochineal and indigo dyes turned the water in the cargo holds murky and burned the divers' eyes. Nevertheless, much of this cargo was also recovered, dried, and shipped back to Havana.

One ship remained missing. A lone survivor reported that she had sunk. Using grapnels and long bights of chain, the salvage vessels began dragging the bottom to find her. In January 1734, they were still searching when a vessel from Nassau, sent by the governor to investigate the situation at the wrecks, arrived on the scene. Upon his return, the captain of the

Bahamian vessel reported that "it seemed very indifferent to them (the Spaniards) whether they found her or not."

Salvage efforts continued for at least four years. In all, the salvors recovered treasure worth approximately twelve million pesos. Evidence of the extent to which passengers and crewmen of the flota smuggled gold and silver was shown by the fact that more treasure was recovered than had been recorded on the cargo manifests when the ships left Havana. The recovery of treasure from the 1733 New Spain flota was one of the most effective and successful salvage operations ever undertaken by the Spanish, yet there was still treasure left to be discovered by modern divers some two hundred years later.

The Bahamian Wreckers

For a period of nearly one hundred years before the Americans took possession, the Keys were the province of the Bahamian vessels that went there to hunt turtles, cut hardwood timber, and salvage wrecks. Actually, the story of Bahamian wrecking goes back much further than that. The first wreckers in the Bahamas came from Bermuda in 1648 as members of a group of English Puritans seeking religious freedom. They called themselves the Eleutheran Adventurers and the island on which they settled Eleuthera. When farming failed to provide sufficient subsistence, the seamen, known as "wrackers," turned to salvaging wrecks to help eke out a living. The disposition of goods salvaged from wrecks was governed by strict rules set forth in the Adventurers' *Articles and Orders.* Any guns and ammunition found in the wrecks became the property of the community for its defense. Wrecked ships and goods were sold at auction. The salvors received one-third of the proceeds, the public treasury one-third, and the remaining third was divided among the original settlers or their heirs in equal shares.

Drawn by news of the growing number of wrecks, more Bermudian seamen came to the Bahamas. The island of New Providence, which has a deep, protected harbor, was settled in 1656 and eventually became the capital of the Bahamas. Judging by the comments of John Oldmixon, a visitor to the islands around 1740, the rules of the *Articles and Orders* had been pretty well forgotten by the time of his visit. Oldmixon wrote, "As for Wrecks, the People of Providence, Harbour Island, and Eleuthera dealt in them as it is said the good Men of Sussex do: All that came ashore was Prize and if a Sailor had, by better Luck than the rest, got ashore as well as his Wreck, he was not sure of getting off again as well. This perhaps is Scandal, but it is most notorious, that the Inhabitants looked upon every Thing they could get out of a Cast-away Ship as their own, and were not at any Trouble to enquire after the Owners."

It is not known when Bahamian vessels began coming to the Keys, but the fact that the Spanish commander of the lost 1733 flota was concerned that Bahamians might attempt to salvage some of the treasure indicates they were already coming to the Keys in the 1730s. Although the Keys were Spanish territory, the authorities in Havana made no serious effort to keep the Bahamians away.

When Spain ceded Florida to England in 1763, the departing Spanish took most, if not all, of the remaining Keys natives with them to Havana. With the threat of attack by the natives eliminated, the number of Bahamian vessels coming to the Keys began to grow.

One year later, a Spanish official on his way from Havana to St. Augustine counted fourteen Bahamian vessels in the Keys. The military governor of East Florida was upset that the Bahamians, despite the fact that they were fellow Englishmen, were trespassing on his territory and taking away valuable turtles, hardwood timber, and wrecked cargoes. He said, "The people from Providence were certain unruly rascals, and that an order would soon have to be sent . . . to seize and punish them." Later, his successor, Governor Grant, a civilian, warned the authorities at Providence that if any one of their vessels hunted turtles and cut timber at the Keys, they ". . . will be prosecuted to the utmost rigor of the law, for committing such trespasses against the Crown." But, in fact, the governor did not have the means to enforce his threat, and the Bahamian turtlers and wreckers continued to come to the Keys in greater numbers.

Lord Dunmore, governor of the Bahamas from 1787 to 1796, had even less respect for his seagoing subjects than did the governors of East Florida. He said, "The lower order of *whites* here being a rather lawless race, the descendants of Pirates, they have not departed from the principles of their ancestors, though their practices may assume the different names of wrecking vessels and Privateers." But the crews of vessels in distress on the reef had a quite different opinion of the merits of the Bahamian wreckers.

In 1770, a British frigate, HMS *Carysfort,* went aground on the reef that still bears her name. Two days after their ship went up on the reef, the crew had the welcome sight of a Bahamian sloop and a Bahamian schooner coming to anchor nearby. The sloop carried out and planted the frigate's bower anchor as a means to haul the ship off, while the schooner carried provisions and other materials ashore to lighten the frigate. By jettisoning guns, cutting away masts, and other extraordinary measures, the frigate's crew finally heaved their vessel afloat the next day.

George Gauld, an English cartographer, surveyed the Keys between 1773 and 1775 to produce accurate charts. In his sailing directions for the Keys, he cautioned shipwrecked mariners to stand by their vessels after going aground to ensure their chances of being rescued by the Bahamian wreckers. He said, "If we consider the activity with which the Wreckers always exert themselves, we must look upon them as a set of very useful men."

The master of the ship *Sophia Bailey,* which ran on the Florida Reef in 1785, had this to say of the Bahamian wrecking captains who got his ship afloat again: "Captain Bell and the rest of the Captains have behaved with the greatest civility; and I shall make it my business to report their friendly conduct to all the underwriters at Lloyd's Coffee-house. You will be pleased to reward them for their trouble."

The Bahamian turtling-wrecking vessels were small sloops or schooners. Their crews–some whites, some free blacks, and some slaves–were men who had been brought up at sea from childhood. As Governor Dunmore noted, some of them were descended from the pirates who ruled Nassau in the early 1700s, and they retained a trace of the outward appearance of their freebooter ancestors by carrying big knives in their belts. One observer described them as "hardy and adventurous Mariners whose power of diving is extraordinary."

For the most part, the turtling-wrecking vessels were owned by the merchants of Nassau. They stocked the vessels with a few barrels of pork and biscuit. The crews were expected to augment their meager supply of provisions by fishing and hunting in the Keys. If there were a large number of wreckers operating from the same harbor, one or two of them might be delegated to fish for the rest. They would, however, receive a share of any salvage that the other vessels obtained. The length of the voyages varied from several weeks to several months, depending on the success the captains had in filling their vessels with salvaged goods, turtles, or hardwood timber.

The captains favored the anchorage at Key Tavernier as a wrecking station because it commanded a view of Carysfort Reef, where the greatest number of wrecks occurred. The anchorage at Indian Key was also much used because of the availability of fresh water from a large sinkhole at the eastern end of nearby Lower Matecumbe Key. The Bahamian vessels also made use of the harbors at Key Biscayne, Bahia Honda, Key Vaca, Big Pine Key, and Key West. In fact, it was the Bahamians who gave Newfound Harbor at Big Pine Key its name. The crews built turtle kraals (pens) in shallow water near shore to hold live turtles, and they may have established temporary facilities on shore for use when hunting deer or when storing salvaged goods. When the captain of a wrecking vessel died in 1804, his crew buried him on Key Tavernier, but there is no evidence the Bahamians ever established permanent settlements on the Keys.

According to the shipping news in the *Bahama Gazette,* during 1790 there were forty arrivals in Nassau of turtling-wrecking vessels from the Florida Keys. Some of these vessels made two, three, or four trips to the Keys during that year. The number of vessels operating in the Keys was not less than twenty-five, of which ten were sloops and fifteen were schooners. Arrival reports for the following year indicate that at least thirty-seven Bahamian vessels, twenty-three sloops, and fourteen schooners had been to the Keys.

The return of Florida to Spain in 1783 had little effect on the activities of the Bahamian vessels operating in the Keys. In 1791, a Spanish *guarda costa* (coast guard vessel) seized two wreckers and took them to Havana. They were detained for two days and released. Two weeks later, an armed schooner flying Spanish colors forced another wrecker to pay a visit to Havana, but there were no further seizures after these two incidents. Apparently, the Spanish authorities realized it was to their advantage to leave the Bahamian wreckers in the Keys alone since their captains made no distinction between English and Spanish ships when it came to rescuing their crews and saving their cargoes.

Proof that there were a large number of Bahamian vessels in the Keys at any single point in time is evidenced by the relatively short interval between the time vessels wrecked on the reef and the time wreckers arrived on the scene to assist them. In 1784, a schooner ran on the reef at midnight. At daylight, three wreckers were standing by to assist. In 1789, a strong current drove a large ship up on the reef where she bilged (had a hole stove in her underwater hull). Before the day was out, several wreckers arrived, took off the passengers and crewmen, and saved part of the cargo. When a fishing vessel ran on the reef off Key Largo the following year, two wreckers arrived the same day and got her off just six hours after she had gone aground. In July 1791, a brig went aground on the reef at eleven o'clock at night. The next morning, twelve wrecking vessels arrived on the scene. Their divers found that the brig had lost her rudder, false keel, and most of her sheathing and was not fit to continue on her voyage. Three of the wrecking vessels took the master, crew, and part of the cargo to Charleston. The others got the brig afloat, made temporary repairs, and brought it to Nassau.

The presence of a number of wreckers in the upper Keys was particularly fortunate for a convoy transiting the Straits of Florida in February 1805. Under the escort of HMS *Fly,* eighteen guns, a group of merchant ships was bound northward through the Straits. At midnight, the leadsman on the *Fly* reported a sounding of twenty fathoms (120 feet). The officer of the watch immediately ordered the helm put up, but it was too late. Three minutes later, the ship struck heavily and plowed through coral heads for a considerable distance. The sea was so rough it was impossible to launch a boat to carry out an anchor. The ship thumped heavily on the coral heads, then bilged and flooded. There was no hope of getting her afloat again. It is illustrative of the uncertainty of navigation of those days that the captain of the *Fly* thought he had run ashore on the Grand Bahama Bank, which was actually some sixty miles to the east. But at daylight, when he saw the low-lying shoreline of Key Largo four or five miles to the west, he knew he had struck Carysfort Reef. At the same time, he saw that two merchant ships of the convoy had also gone hard aground.

Once again, the Bahamian wrecking vessels were on the lookout. As the captain of the *Fly* reported, "We soon had the pleasure of seeing several Providence wreckers standing off to our assistance. . . . Some of the wreckers got to us by eight o'clock [that morning], and, before night, we had got off all the people [the crew], several day's allowance of provisions, and the greatest part of the baggage." For the next two days, the wreckers worked at saving as much of the doomed ships' rigging, sails, and other equipment as they could. They then carried the salvaged materials and crews of the three ships to Nassau.

The methods used by the Bahamians to get ships off the reef and to save their cargoes were much the same as those used by the American wreckers who succeeded them. (These methods are described in detail in Chapter 6.) There was, however, one technique used by the Bahamian divers that was apparently not adopted by the Americans. According to a Bahamian historian, in 1687 Bahamian salvage divers were using an inverted cask with air trapped inside it to prolong their working time underwater.

The captain of an English ship lost on Ledbury Reef off the upper Keys in 1790 reported that he observed wreckers setting fire to a ship ashore some distance away. The reporter who wrote this news item claimed that the wreckers set fire to wrecks so that they would not serve to warn other ships off the reef. It is apparent that he knew nothing about salvage methods. When a ship was a total loss, the wreckers might set fire to it in order to obtain easier access to the lower cargo holds or to make it easier to recover metal parts such as copper sheathing and iron chain plates.

Another writer, who rode a Bahamian wrecker in the early 1800s, reported the following conversation with the ship's captain:

> Writer: What success in cruising?
> Captain: Middling–but middling.
> Writer: We have seen very few wreckers to the eastward–are there many to the westward?
> Captain: We lay with forty sail four months along Florida shores.
> Writer: Forty sails? Then certainly you must have had many opportunities of being essentially serviceable to

vessels passing the Gulf stream, by directing them to keep off places of danger, with which you made it your business to become acquainted?

Captain: Not much of that–they went on generally in the night.

Writer: But then you might have afforded them timely notice, by making beacons on shore, or showing your lights?

Captain: No, no [laughing]; we always put them out for a better chance by night.

Writer: But would there not have been more humanity in showing them their danger?

Captain: I did not go there for humanity; I went wracking.

Bahamian wreckers were a godsend to shipwrecked mariners on the Florida reef.
(From the collections of The Mariners' Museum, Newport News, Virginia)

The questions and answers were undoubtedly made partly in jest, but the tendency to malign the motives of the wreckers was a common one among persons who had no firsthand knowledge of what they did. When Lt. Matthew C. Perry, USN, took possession of Key West for the United States in 1822, he wrote the secretary of the Navy, "Heretofore the Florida Keys have been the resort of smuglers [sic], New Providence wreckers, and in fact a Set of desperadoes who have paid but little regard to either Law or Honesty. . . ."

While denunciations of Bahamian wreckers in the 1600s as rascals, descendants of pirates, and members of a lawless race may have had some element of truth, by the end of the eighteenth century, such labels no longer applied. Two articles in Bahamian newspapers shed a new light on their character.

A writer who called himself "A Friend to the Truth" had this to say in the *Royal Gazette* on August 13, 1806: "The *Natives of the Bahamas* have always as far as ever came to my knowledge, acted with Honor and Honesty to those unfortunate persons who wrecked among them; and the universal practice is, to appoint indifferent persons to say what they ought to be entitled to for their services; by which a number of lives and considerable property are saved. . . ."

In the *Royal Gazette* on March 21, 1817, another favorable evaluation of the wreckers appeared: "The boisterous weather experienced from the 4th to the 14th instant has caused the loss of several vessels among our reefs and banks; and our wreckers have evinced further proofs of their ready exertions in behalf of the unfortunate. Whatever may be imputed by the unbanded and illiberal to the adventurous pursuits of these hardy people, it is impossible to withhold from them the credit and praise of being most useful in their avocations to the interest of humanity, as well in the preservation of property as in the rescue of their fellow creatures from destruction."

As the years passed and the traffic through the Straits of Florida increased, the Bahamian vessels in the Keys turned more and more to wrecking and less and less to turtling and cutting timber. As early as 1769, it was reported that most of the valuable hardwood timber in the Keys had been cut. When the United States acquired the Louisiana Territory in 1803 and more ports were established along the Gulf coast, the increase in shipping traffic and wrecks accelerated. By 1816, ships were running up on the reef at a rate greater than one a month.

The wreckers brought their salvaged cargoes to Nassau, where the goods were sold at auction. Customs duties took fifteen percent, and the governor received a tithe. On goods not claimed by owners, the Vice Admiralty Court took thirty percent. After the end of the War of 1812, the annual revenue from duties, estimated at fifteen thousand pounds sterling, became the principal means of economic support for the town of Nassau.

Salvage awards to the wrecking vessel ranged from between forty to sixty percent of the net value of the cargo saved. Half of this went to the owner and half to the crew, divided into shares according to an agreement drawn up for the voyage. Although wreck salvaging has generally been viewed as a very lucrative occupation, this was not true for the crewmen. According to one Bahamian historian's analysis, a wrecking crewman's average take was less than the wage of a common laborer.

The Bahamian wreckers operating along the Florida Reef in the early 1800s faced even greater dangers than the hazards of maneuvering a small sailing vessel alongside a wrecked ship on the reef in the middle of a howling gale. There was an ever-present threat of being attacked and robbed by pirates or, in time of war, having their vessel seized by enemy privateers. In July 1804, a heavily armed French privateer with a large crew captured three Bahamian wrecking vessels at Key Tavernier and sank two of them. The crew of one of the wreckers escaped ashore in their boats. The other two crews were taken prisoner and carried away aboard the remaining wrecker. Members of the escaped crew said they did not have sufficient guns and ammunition to fight the privateer off.

The following year, another French privateer captured three wrecking vessels in the Straits off Key Largo. Two other wreckers in the vicinity outsailed the privateer and escaped. The French crew robbed the wrecking captains of their clothes and valuables and kept their slaves but let one of the wrecking vessels go free to carry the Bahamian crews back to Nassau.

With the end of the Napoleonic Wars and the War of 1812, thousands of seamen on men-of-war and privateers were thrown out of work, and many of them turned to piracy. Pirate vessels operated from the northern coast of Cuba and the more remote islands of the Bahamas, but some of their activity spilled over into the Straits of Florida and along the Keys. Perhaps because Bahamian wrecking vessels were not considered particularly lucrative targets, reports of attacks on them are few and, unlike most other pirate attacks, did not result in bloodshed.

Two Bahamian wreckers were assisting an American brig, ashore on the reef in 1819, when a band of eighteen pirates in a small sloop and a boat arrived on the scene. They boarded the brig, ordered the wrecking captains off, then proceeded to rob the passengers. But these pirates were quite different from the usual gang of bloodthirsty cutthroats who preyed on defenseless ships. They did not harm anyone on the brig or either of the wrecking vessels. The captain of one of the wreckers said they treated him politely and took nothing. The captain of the other said they took only a barrel of flour, a spyglass, and several small articles. Later that same year, a sixteen-gun pirate brig flying Spanish colors chased and boarded a Bahamian sloop returning from the Keys. They robbed the crewmen of a number of small articles and took away some fresh fish they had caught but did not molest anyone.

The crew of the Bahamian sloop *Whim* did not fare quite so well in 1824. Commodore Porter's antipiracy squadron, based at Key West, had been in operation for a year, but a few pirates still eluded his pirate hunters. The *Whim* was under way off Cape Florida when she was chased by a *felucca* (small, lateen-rigged, galley-type vessel). The Bahamians ran their sloop ashore and escaped, but the pirates plundered their vessel and sank it as well as another Spanish sloop that was nearby. The crews of both vessels obtained a boat at Cape Florida and made their way to Key West. One of Porter's schooners immediately got under way to search for the felucca but failed to find her.

Some of the Bahamian sloops and schooners did not confine their activities along the Florida coast to wrecking and turtling. In wartime, some of them turned to privateering as a more lucrative occupation. Others took up carrying cargo and trading when wrecks were scarce. One of these was the schooner *Chance* of Nassau, owned by Alexander Arbuthnot, a merchant, and captained by Lewis Fenix. Arbuthnot had established a trading post at the mouth of the Suwannee River on the west coast of Florida and was furnishing the Seminole Indians with gunpowder, cloth, and other manufactured goods in exchange for fur, hides, corn, and beeswax. When General Andrew Jackson invaded northern Florida in 1818, his troops captured Arbuthnot and Fenix as well as Robert Ambrister, a commissioned officer in the Royal Colonial Marines, also from New Providence. Ambrister was involved in a scheme to seize Florida from the Spanish. Jackson convened a summary court-martial that found Arbuthnot and Ambrister guilty of inciting the Indians to war against the United States. Arbuthnot was hanged from the yardarm of the *Chance*, and Ambrister was shot by a firing squad. The fate of wrecking captain Fenix is unknown.

Survivors of shipwrecks were not the only passengers Bahamian wreckers brought back from the Keys. When General Jackson's troops destroyed Seminole Indian villages in north Florida in 1818, the Indians and the runaway slaves who were living with them fled south. Some of the blacks fled all the way to Biscayne Bay and the Keys with the hope of escaping to the Bahamas. The black crewmembers of the Bahamian wreckers sympathized with the starving runaways and persuaded their captains to carry them to the Bahamas, where they were deposited on some of the more remote islands. More escaped slaves are known to have made their way to the Keys after news of the 1819 treaty transferring Florida to the United States (thereby making it slave territory) came to their knowledge. A letter written by the governor of Florida in 1823 stated that at least ninety Negroes had reached the lower Keys, where they were waiting for Bahamian wreckers to carry them away. Today, descendants of those ex-slaves brought to the Bahamas by the wreckers can still be found on Andros Island.

A Bahamian wrecking schooner brought another unusual group of passengers from the Keys to Nassau in October 1819. It was a party of twenty-eight Muscogulge Indians (Muskogee-speaking Indians of the Creek Confederation). During the War of 1812, they had been allies of the British and had been promised protection by the British military commanders at the battle of New Orleans. Since then, their tribe, some two thousand in number, had been driven from their homes into Florida by the Coweta Indians, who were encouraged and financed to do so by the American government. Hunted like wild deer, the Indians were now starving. Their chiefs had come to Nassau hoping to get supplies from the British government.

Although the Bahamian authorities sympathized with the Indians, they were unwilling to provide any aid for fear of upsetting peaceful relations with the U.S. government. After a ten-day stay, during which they were housed and fed, the authorities engaged a wrecking schooner to carry the delegation back to Key Tavernier.

The Americans Move In

After the end of the War of 1812, New England fishermen began extending their operations to the Carolina and Florida coasts in the winter. They would sell their catches of grouper and snapper at Charleston, Savannah, Havana, and in the Bahamas. The Havana market fishery soon became the most profitable portion of the so-called southern, or winter, fisheries. Sloop-rigged smacks would fish along the Keys and, when their live wells were full, take their catch to Havana, usually not more than a day's sail away. An added advantage of this fishery was the opportunity to salvage wrecks along the reef when the occasion arose. The majority of the fishing-wrecking smacks in the Keys were from Connecticut, particularly the New London–Mystic area.

Despite the transfer of Florida to the United States and the increasing presence of American vessels in the Keys, the Bahamians not only remained but increased their numbers. They were determined to maintain their hold on the lucrative salvage business there. Between the time the treaty of cession was signed in 1819 and the time Americans settled Key West in 1822, there were no conflicts between the American and Bahamian vessels in the Keys. In a few instances, American and Bahamian vessels salvaged cargo from the same wreck without incident. But in December 1821, the grand jury of East Florida complained that the Keys had become "the resort of wreckers [Bahamians] and pirates" and recommended that a naval and military force be stationed there "for the purpose of suppressing those disorders." In March 1822, the governor of Florida wrote the secretary of state that from thirty-seven to forty Bahamian wreckers were operating in the Keys, not only salvaging wrecks but "taking quantities of the finest Turtles." He proposed that wrecking, turtling, and fishing in the Keys be placed on a basis "to ensure a monopoly or first preference to our own citizens." He also recommended that a military post be established at Key West.

That same month, the U.S. Revenue Cutter *Alabama* boarded two Bahamian wreckers in the Keys and examined their papers. The *Alabama's* officers treated the Bahamians politely and requested one of the captains to pilot them to Cape Florida. On arrival there, the cutter's officers arrested a settler named Levi James on charges of piracy. In retaliation for having guided the cutter to his home, James told the cutter's captain that the two Bahamian captains had transported runaway slaves from the Keys to the Bahamas. Upon hearing this, the captain of the *Alabama* placed the two captains under arrest and escorted them to Mobile. After a brief stay, the authorities at Mobile released the wreckers without trial. Apparently there was no evidence to substantiate the charge of helping slaves to escape.

In the meantime, a letter from an official at Key West to the Bahamian government explained that the two wreckers were detained not because they had aided runaway slaves, but because they had Negro slaves on board while they were in U.S. waters, even though the slaves were members of the crew. The letter explained that the U.S. government had not as yet issued any orders to prevent Bahamian vessels from operating along the Florida coast, and that they were welcome as long as their crews did not include any slaves. Upon learning this, the Nassau newspaper warned all wrecking and turtling vessels planning to go to Florida to carry a list of their crewmen, certified by a customs official, so as to eliminate any suspicion of an intent to land slaves in the United States.

When, in April 1822, a Bahamian wrecker arrived at a wrecked French brig on the reef, the captain found that two American vessels were already there and had offloaded the brig's cargo of logwood. One of the American captains told the Bahamians that a U.S. Navy warship would soon arrive on the reef to prevent Bahamian vessels from coming any closer to the coast than one league (about three miles). Despite this warning, which had no basis in fact, and the previous seizure of two of their fellow captains by a revenue cutter, the Bahamians continued to operate in the Keys and render valuable assistance to vessels in distress.

One of the vessels aided by the Bahamians, not once but twice, was the United States Schooner *Alligator,* a member of the antipiracy squadron. In March 1822, the captain of the *Alligator* asked the captain of the Bahamian wrecking sloop *Fox* to aid him in hunting pirates along the Cuban coast. During a subsequent engagement with pirates, the Bahamian captain was wounded, and his sloop robbed. He claimed that the fight with the pirates was lost because of the cowardice of the American sailors stationed aboard his sloop. He was, however, reimbursed by the *Alligator*'s captain for the articles that had been stolen.

Seven months later, the *Alligator* was returning from a battle with pirates on the Cuban coast, during which her captain had been killed. During the night, she wrecked on that portion of the reef that bears her name today and was a total loss. Once again, a Bahamian wrecker came to the aid of the *Alligator* by taking aboard the most valuable articles from the schooner before her captain blew her up.

In a letter written in May 1823, John DuBose, inspector of customs at St. Augustine, proposed measures to ensure that the U.S. government would receive payment of duties on goods salvaged from wrecks on the Florida reef. He said that the Bahamian wreckers "consider it [wreck salvaging on the Florida reef] their right, and are determined to persevere in it, until our Government, by the adoption of some energetick [sic] Measures Shall Compel them to withdraw–The extent of this trade [wreck salvaging] and the very Serious injury done to the Revenue of the Ud. States by the English Wreckers, may be estimated by the number of Vessels employed in it [which he reported as 120 sail vessels]–and also by the amount of Duties paid by them to the Custom House in Nassau."

After the settlement of Key West in 1822, more and more American vessels, many of them from New England, came to the Keys to salvage wrecks, and some of their captains and owners settled there. The American captains did everything they could, short of outright force, to make the Bahamians unwelcome. They avoided any friendly association, refused to furnish them provisions or assistance, and deliberately ran their vessels into near collision with any Bahamian vessels they met. Government officials rigorously enforced revenue laws relating to foreign vessels in United States waters. Finally, in 1825, the Key West wrecking vessel owners and merchants succeeded in persuading Congress to pass a law that effectively excluded the Bahamians from salvaging wrecks in the Keys. The law required that all property salvaged in U.S. waters be brought to an

American port of entry, and made any vessel that took such cargo to a foreign port subject to seizure and condemnation.

With the passage of this law, the Bahamian wreckers left the Keys, but not forever. Their experience on the reef taught them that the opportunities for making money from salvaging wrecks were much better in the Keys than in the Bahamas. By the 1830s, many of them were back on the reef, having immigrated to the Keys with their families and become U.S. citizens.

Chapter 2

Storm driving a ship onto the Florida Reef (From the collections of the Mariners' Museum, Newport News, Virginia)

KEY WEST BECOMES A WRECKING CENTER AND SEAPORT

Strategic and Commercial Advantages

Commodore David Porter, USN, a hero of the War of 1812, commanded the Navy's antipiracy squadron at Key West from 1823 to 1825. In discussing the strategic importance of the island, he observed that Key West "is to the Gulf of Mexico what Gibraltar is to the Mediterranean." In a letter to the secretary of the Navy written in 1829, he outlined Key West's advantages as a naval station as follows:

1. It commands the outlet of all trade from Jamaica, the Caribbean Sea, the Bay of Honduras, and the Gulf of Mexico.
2. It protects the outlet and inlet of all the trade of the Gulf of Mexico, the whole western country of Louisiana and Florida.
3. It holds in subjection the trade of Cuba.
4. It is a check to the naval forces of whatever nation may possess Cuba.

From a commercial point of view, he commented, its closeness to Havana "would provide a ready market for salvaged cargoes," and its excellent harbor "would furnish a convenient stopover for vessels bound to and from the Gulf of Mexico, Bay of Honduras, and the coasts of Louisiana and Florida."

In spite of these military and commercial advantages, Key West and the rest of the Keys remained unsettled (except for the native Americans) and unfortified for three hundred years after they were discovered by Europeans. As early as 1569, an official in Havana appealed to the King of Spain to authorize a military post in the Keys to protect Spanish shipping moving through the Straits. In 1766, when Florida was English territory, the governor of East Florida proposed establishment of a settlement at Key West to preserve the resources of the Keys from the incursions of the Bahamians and the Cubans and to furnish prompt aid to the crews of wrecked ships. But neither the Spanish nor the English government could be persuaded that the Keys were of sufficient strategic or economic importance to justify the cost of fortifications or settlements.

When it became apparent that Florida would become United States territory, two American businessmen, John W. Simonton and John Whitehead, recognized the commercial and military possibilities of Key West and took steps to take advantage of them. Simonton, with business interests in Mobile, Havana, and New York, became familiar with the Keys as a result of passing by them a number of times on voyages between the East Coast, Cuba, and the Gulf Coast. Whitehead, after being shipwrecked on the Bahamas Bank in 1818, had continued his voyage to Mobile in another vessel, which stopped at Key West. Impressed by the excellent harbor, he undoubtedly communicated his impressions to his friend Simonton on arrival in Mobile. The two businessmen visualized the island, with its fine harbor fronting a steady flow of shipping traffic, as an ideal location for a wrecking vessel station and a depot for salvaged cargoes. They also saw an opportunity to reap profits by providing supplies and services to the passing ships, as well as to any naval forces that might be stationed at the island.

Florida became U.S. territory in 1821. During a business trip to Havana in January 1822, Simonton purchased a claim to the island from its Spanish owner for $2,000. Soon thereafter, he divided his interest into four parts and sold three of them to business associates, one of whom was Whitehead. Two weeks prior to completing the purchase, he sent a letter to the secretary of the Navy promoting Key West as the ideal location for a naval depot. In a memorandum, which was forwarded to the secretary of the Treasury, he wrote that the island was the "only eligible situation for a depot for wrecked property on the whole coast of Florida. . . . If this place was made a Port of Entry it would in all probability become a place of deposit for the productions of other Countries particularly that of Great Britain and France, as it may be termed a key for the whole of the Bay of Mexico [Gulf of Mexico] and the north side of the Island of Cuba." Once it became a port of entry, he predicted, merchants would establish themselves there and build warehouses to receive cargoes salvaged from wrecked ships.

Simonton's letter was not the only one the secretary of the Navy received extolling Key West's advantageous situation. Lt. Matthew C. Perry, USN, commanding the U.S. Schooner *Shark*, was ordered to proceed to Key West, take possession of the island and examine its situation as a site for a naval depot. On March 25, 1822, Perry planted the U.S. flag on Key West with a handful of newly arrived settlers looking on. In his report to the secretary of the Navy, Perry said he had "come to the conclusion that it [Key West] possesses many advantages as a Naval Rendezvous." In a war, he observed, "undisputed possession of the Florida Keys will be a matter of great importance as it will insure undisturbed Navigation of the NW side of the Florida Stream (or Gulf of Florida) [the Florida Straits] to our Merchant Vessels." He also noted that its location midway between Florida and Cuba and between the East and Gulf coasts of the U.S. had "induced many to believe that in the course of time, the Island must become a place of considerable commerce."

Growth of a Seaport

What attracted Porter, Simonton, Whitehead, Perry, and others to Key West, in addition to its strategic position, was its fine harbor. Porter remarked that it was the "best harbor, within the limits of the United States or its territories, south of the Chesapeake." It was deep enough and large enough to accommodate the Navy's largest ships. It was protected in all directions except from the southwest, from which storm winds seldom blew. Three natural channels furnished access from the south, the southwest, and the northwest. As a result, sailing ships could enter the harbor in almost any wind. In the inner harbor, the water was deep close to the shore, which greatly facilitated the construction of wharves for deep-draft ships.

Simonton's letters, memorials, and influence paid off when, on May 7, 1822, Congress created a new district for customs collection covering the southern Florida coast. Soon thereafter, President James Monroe designated Key West as the port of entry for the new district and appointed a collector of customs. This meant that wrecked goods from foreign countries, with payment of duties, could be landed in Key West rather than be carried to the next nearest port of entry, St. Augustine. In the meantime, employees of the island's new owners had been at work clearing the land along the waterfront and constructing wharves and warehouses to be ready to receive salvaged cargoes. They had also cut and stockpiled wood and imported sheep and hogs to be held for sale to ships calling at the port. Their progress was interrupted, however, when, in April 1823, Commodore Porter and the antipiracy squadron arrived and made the island their headquarters. Because Simonton's purchase was in dispute, Porter considered the whole island to be U.S. Government property. His carpenters built storehouses and workshops on choice waterfront lots that the owners had reserved for themselves. He dictated where the property owners could build and even gave permission to others to build on their lots without recompense. His sailors appropriated the wood, sheep, and hogs without payment. In effect, Porter declared martial law.

Nevertheless, under the protection from pirates provided by the squadron, Key West began to come into its own as a seaport. In May 1823, Porter wrote, "The arrivals and departures of the American vessels from the port of Havana alone average about thirty a week, and those from Matanzas about twenty. Not a day elapses but that great numbers of American vessels are to be met passing through the gulf [Straits of Florida], and since our establishment here, they daily in numbers pass in sight of us."

News of the profits to be made from the ships piling up on the reef drew American vessels from Atlantic ports, particularly New England, to make wrecking voyages to the Keys. A number of the captains stayed on and became permanent residents of Key West.

When Porter was ordered north to face a court of inquiry in February 1825, the property owners and merchants rejoiced, and construction of waterfront facilities moved ahead to accommodate the increasing number of wrecked ships and salvaged cargoes being brought into port. A correspondent for the *East Florida Herald* wrote in April 1825: "Notwithstanding the local situation of Key West being unfavorable to health, yet there is, from a variety of circumstances, a great field for industry and enterprize. The place is rapidly improving. Very extensive Warehouses are building–roads are cutting in different directions and enterprizing merchants are locating there."

Simonton reported, "From December 1824 to December 1825, $293,353.00 worth of wrecked property was sold here." American fishing smacks operating out of Key West and fishing for the Havana market numbered approximately thirty in 1825. These smacks also salvaged wrecks when the opportunity arose.

As shipping traffic through the Straits of Florida increased, so did the number of arrivals and departures from the port of Key West. Simonton, in 1828, estimated that two hundred vessels entered the port annually. By 1835, on average, one vessel was entering port and one was leaving almost

Key West in 1838 looking north. Large buildings along waterfront are merchants' warehouses for storing salvaged cargoes.
(from a sketch by W. A. Whitehead, courtesy of Monroe County Public Library)

every day. In the early 1830s, sixty to ninety percent of all imports and exports of the Territory of Florida entered or cleared through Key West customs. In March 1848, a Key West lawyer, William R. Hackley, recorded in his diary, "A number of vessels bound east have passed in sight, nineteen were in sight at one time yesterday." Following the discovery of gold in California in 1849, steamers carrying prospectors to Central American ports for overland transport to Pacific ports would stop in Key West for water, coal, provisions, and repairs. During the 1850s, Key West became a junction point on mail-steamer routes to and from Gulf coast and Cuban ports.

The growth in shipping calling at the port created the need for more and improved shoreside facilities such as wharves, warehouses, chandleries, sail lofts, and shipwright shops. In the 1830s, there were three warehouses and three wharves capable of berthing large ships. By 1851, with the town's population approaching three thousand, there were ten warehouses, eleven wharves of varying capacities, and four lookout towers erected by individual merchants. The towers were used for sighting incoming and passing vessels and reading signals from them, as well as for sighting wrecks on the reef off Key West. The merchants, who owned the wharfs and warehouses and were the chief beneficiaries of the wrecking business, were determined not to let any newcomers siphon off any of their profits. The lawyer Hackley wrote in his diary in 1853, "All of the merchants being in partnership, or rather have made an arrangement to divide the wharfage, storage, and commissions [as agents for salvaged cargoes] among themselves. What that is I do not know as the arrangement is kept secret. [They] have also purchased the whole of the water lots to prevent anyone from building other wharfs and opposing them in the business."

Up until 1834, vessels arriving at Key West in need of bottom scraping and painting or repair had to be careened, that is, heaved down alongside a dock or on the beach. This was a laborious, time-consuming, and hazardous process. In November 1834, the *Key West Enquirer* reported that an "old resident has returned to Key West bringing with him a rail way for the hauling up of vessels. Something of this sort was much wanted here, and we can see no way in which it can fail to be one of the greatest improvements that could have taken place." The paper failed to mention

Key West waterfront in 1855: salvaged brig undergoing repair in foreground, schooner careened at wharf to repair or clean underwater hull, lookout towers atop merchants' warehouses (J. C. Clapp, lithograph of Chandlor and Co. From the collections of The Mariners' Museum, Newport News, Virginia)

how large a vessel the railway could accommodate, but its capacity was undoubtedly quite limited. In 1853, the firm of Bowne and Curry, principal merchants of the town, constructed a marine railway capable of hauling vessels up to one hundred tons and in 1859 enlarged it to a capacity of five hundred tons with steam power.

There were no provisions for the care of sick, injured, or shipwrecked seamen arriving in Key West. They were generally taken into private homes by compassionate citizens and supported by charitable donations. A bill providing for the medical care of seamen in hospitals to be built at the country's principal seaports had been passed by Congress in 1798. These hospitals, called marine hospitals, were constructed and supported by money deducted from the wages of seamen. At the urging of leading citizens, Congress authorized the construction of a marine hospital at Key West in 1844. The hospital was completed in 1845, continued in operation until 1943, and, from time to time, provided medical care to military personnel as well as merchant seamen.

Rival Wrecking Stations

Although Key West was by far the largest and most active wrecking station in the Keys, it was not the only one. At Cape Florida, on the southern tip of Key Biscayne, there were three captains who salvaged wrecks in that area when the occasion arose. They were members of families who had settled at the mouth of the Miami River around 1810.

In November 1822, the same year that Key West was settled, two wrecking captains, Joshua Appleby and John Fiveash, established a rival wrecking station on Knight Key at the western end of Key Vaca. They named their tiny settlement Port Monroe and sent notices to newspapers to attract business. The announcements stated that Port Monroe "has the advantages of a large and spacious harbor and the proprietors are furnished with experienced pilots, good vessels, boats, and provisions of all kinds to relieve those who may be so unfortunate as to get on the Florida Reef. . . . We are determined that nothing on our part (that attention and industry will ensure) will be neglected for the immediate relief of the unfortunate stranger."

Most of Appleby's attention and industry, however, were devoted to prosecuting a scheme he had concocted in partnership with the captain of a Colombian privateer. To avoid the necessity of sending captured ships back to Colombia for adjudication by an admiralty court, the captain of the privateer would deliberately wreck them on the reef and sell their cargoes to Appleby. Appleby would then salvage the cargoes and ship them north to be resold for a handsome profit. This operation was a violation of both international law and U.S. customs regulations. When Commodore Porter got word of it at Key West, he had Appleby arrested. Although Appleby was later released, the Port Monroe wrecking settlement soon faded from existence.

Not long after the demise of Port Monroe, another settlement was made by a few wreckers on the eastern end of Key Vaca. By 1836, there were about a dozen families, among them the family of William H. Bethel, one of the most successful wrecking captains on the reef. (The story of his wrecking career is told in Chapter 5.) The population, mostly Bahamian, grew until, by 1840, there were nearly two hundred settlers on the island. However, most were farmers and fishermen. When, in 1840, during the

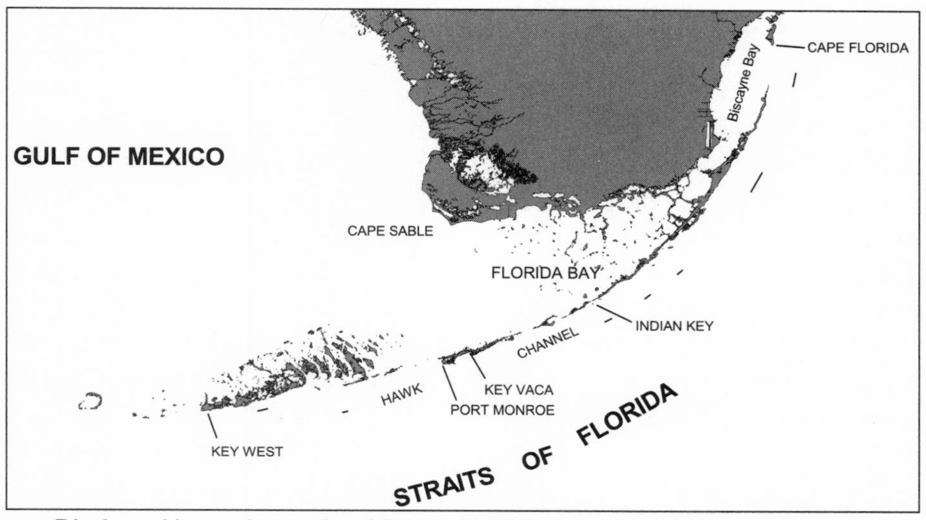

Rival wrecking stations at Port Monroe, Key Vaca, Indian Key, and Cape Florida.
(drawing by Erich Mueller)

Second Seminole War, a party of warriors attacked and destroyed the settlement on Indian Key, nearly all the settlers on Key Vaca fled to Key West. The island never again assumed any importance as a wrecking station.

The biggest rival to the Key West wrecking establishment sprang up on a tiny eleven-acre island some seventy miles from Key West named Indian Key. Located about a half mile offshore of Lower Matecumbe Key, the island was often visited by wreckers. It was only thirty-five miles from Carysfort Reef, where the great majority of wrecks occurred, and directly opposite Alligator Reef, another dangerous part of the reef. A principal attraction to the wreckers was the ready availability of fresh water from several large sinkholes on the eastern end of Lower Matecumbe Key. The island also had a reputation for being relatively mosquito free. Indian Key became even more attractive when, in 1824, Appleby, in partnership with another resident of Port Monroe, underwrote the construction of a store on the island. The store carried supplies and provisions needed by the wrecking vessels and also did a brisk trade with settlers and Indians from the Biscayne Bay area. Soon, wreckers began building homes for their families on the island. When Dr. Strobel, a Key West physician, stopped at the island in 1829, the residents invited him to attend a "ball" in a large building. Strobel described his evening as follows: "The ball room was a kind of piazza, or outshot [sic] from the main building; it was neither lathed nor plastered, but was well lit up. The company consisted of ten or twelve well dressed, decent looking females, who were either wives or daughters of the wreckers and turtlers. Some of these had brought their children, clean, chubby-faced, hearty little dogs. There was also present a dozen or more seafaring men, having on their best suits; they were dressed in clean round jackets and pantaloons, white shirts, silk stockings, and pumps."

Ownership of the store, which was apparently turning a good profit, changed hands several times. In 1828, it was purchased by Thomas Gibson. Sometime between that purchase and 1831, Gibson constructed a two-story building, which was used as a kind of a hotel. For entertainment of the guests, mostly crewmen from wrecking vessels, it included a nine-pin bowling alley and a billiard room.

Thus, the settlement on Indian Key was a growing enterprise when, in 1831, an ambitious and unprincipled young wrecking captain named Jacob Housman decided it was the ideal place to create his own wrecking center free from the domination of the merchants of Key West. For five thousand dollars, Housman purchased from Thomas Gibson "all that piece, parcel, and Island of land situated in the County of Monroe . . . and called Indian Key." Included in the purchase was the "kind of hotel," with its bowling alley and billiard room, and the store. Over the next few years, with profits from wreck salvaging and from the store, Housman developed the island into a beautiful tropical village and a well-equipped wrecking port. He laid out the streets, built houses for his employees and slaves, imported rich soil, and planted various tropical plants and fruits. To serve the wrecking vessels, he constructed three wharves, two warehouses, and large cisterns for storing fresh water. He built workshops and employed a blacksmith, shipwrights, and other skilled craftsmen to maintain and repair wrecking vessels. The full story of Jacob Housman's checkered wrecking career, the creation of his private wrecking empire on Indian Key, and the ultimate destruction of that empire in the Seminole Indian raid of 1840 is told in Chapter 8.

Chapter 3

American merchant ship *Sierra Nevada*, wrecked off Key Largo in 1858. Seven wrecking vessels with ninety-two crewmen got her off in thirty-six hours. Salvage award: $17,000
(oil painting by unknown Chinese artist. From the collections of The Mariners' Museum, Newport News, Virginia)

THE WRECKING BUSINESS

Settlement of Salvage Claims

At first, Keys wreckers settled their salvage claims either by direct negotiation with the master of the wrecked ship or by mutual agreement with the master to submit the claim to local arbitration. Failing that, the wrecking captain could file a claim for salvage against the owners and underwriters in the superior court at St. Augustine. In mid-1823, the Florida Territorial Legislative Council passed an act to govern the settlement of salvage claims. It required that wreckers bringing wrecked property to port inform the local justice of the peace or notary public. That official would then appoint a five-man jury to decide the salvage claim. The ship's owner or master would select two of the jurors, the salvors would select two, and the justice of the peace or notary would select the fifth juror and preside over the proceedings. As it was almost impossible to find anyone in Key West who did not derive an income either directly or indirectly from wrecking, the juries made outrageously high awards, ranging from seventy-five to ninety-five percent of the value of the cargo saved. The *Pensacola Gazette* of August 20, 1825, reported that in a salvage case decided under the territorial law, "The presiding magistrate was the judge who condemned–the auctioneer who sold–and the purchaser at the sale of some of the [salvaged] property." A letter writer to the *East Florida Herald* wrote in 1825, "It will be seen that the property falling into their hands [the Florida wreckers] is almost wholly appropriated to their own use. In many cases where considerable property has been saved, it would have been as well for the owners and underwriters had the same been totally lost or have fallen into the hands of pirates."

The Key West jury awards enraged shipping owners and underwriters. An article in the *Newport Mercury* on November 12, 1825, reported, "Great complaints are now made, particularly by underwriters, respecting the conduct of the Florida wreckers in consequence of the exorbitant salvage usually allowed them under the law of the territorial government. It is frequently the case that nothing is left after the payment of salvage for either underwriters or owners. It is the general opinion among the well informed lawyers in Florida that the law is unconstitutional and that it will be repealed at the next session of the legislative council."

In fact, the law had already been declared unconstitutional by the judge of the superior court in St. Augustine after hearing a suit against a jury-decreed salvage award of ninety-five percent. Soon thereafter, in February 1826, Congress annulled the law. The wrecking community returned to arbitration as the principal means of settlement, but the awards continued to be unreasonably high. In May 1826, the *Savannah Georgian* reported two awards by arbitration of seventy-five and eighty percent. Another news item that same month reported that a small sloop with a crew of six, working for just three days, salvaged one hundred bales of cotton and demanded an award of $5,000. The insurance companies objected but could do nothing unless a salvor or a buyer of wrecked property happened to come within the jurisdiction of a federal court where he could be sued. A congressman was so incensed at the high awards that he offered a resolution to discontinue Key West as a port of entry. However, nothing came of it.

The Florida legislative council petitioned Congress to establish a federal court in Key West to take over settlement of salvage claims. Surprisingly, the merchants and wreckers of Key West also sent memorials to Congress supporting creation of a court with admiralty jurisdiction at

Key West. A memorial prepared by Simonton read in part:

> Heretofore, for the want of a court, the parties interested have consented to refer the matter to arbitration, and thereby to have the salvage ascertained; this most certainly they had not merely the power, but the right to do. If, as is alleged to be the case, higher rates of allowance [salvage awards] have been made, than was required by the risks and labor encountered in rescuing the property, it only proves the necessity of creating a tribunal clothed with government sanction, that thereby such errors may for the future be prevented or avoided.

Another memorial signed by forty-seven wrecking captains and wrecking vessel owners pointed out that the nearest federal court at St. Augustine was 450 miles away, and that carrying wrecked property there "would be attended with great delay, risk, and Trouble, and in many instances could not be carried there at all, on account of the perishable state in which it is frequently found." The wreckers were also concerned that "at present when Property is saved, there is no Tribunal on the Coast that has any control over it, and it can be carried away by the Owners, in defiance of any thing that can be done by the Salvors or Inhabitants, as has already been the case in some instances." Congress listened and, in May 1828, established the Superior Court of the Southern Judicial District of the Territory of Florida at Key West with admiralty jurisdiction. In 1847, two years after Florida became a state, it was replaced by the District Court of the United States for the Southern District of Florida. The court was to have two regular sessions each year but would be open at all times for admiralty cases (provided the judge was present). The Key West court was the only court in the United States authorized to license wrecking captains and wrecking vessels and to revoke such licenses for misconduct. James Webb served as the first judge until his resignation in 1839, when he was succeeded by William Marvin. Marvin served as territorial judge until 1845 and as district judge from 1847 to 1863 and wrote the authoritative work on salvage law titled *A Treatise on the Law of Wreck and Salvage*. The first term of the

Judge James Webb, first judge of the Superior Court ("wrecking court") at Key West from 1828 to 1839 (courtesy of Monroe County Public Library)

court commenced in November 1828, and almost simultaneously, the Key West newspaper, the *Register,* announced the arrival of a vessel with "an assorted cargo and *seven lawyers*."

Grounds for revoking a wrecker's license were embezzlement of wrecked goods, voluntarily running a vessel aground while piloting her, collusion with the master of a wreck, or corruption of the master by an unlawful present or promise. If the misconduct was not sufficient to warrant taking away a wrecker's license, the judge could decree partial or total forfeiture of his salvage award. In 1847, Congress strengthened the court's control of wreckers with the additional requirement that their vessels be seaworthy and properly equipped for salvage operations.

Even after the federal court was established, there was no legal requirement that salvage claims be submitted to the court. In certain situations, the master of the wrecked vessel might agree to pay the wrecker a fixed fee for getting his ship off the reef. Most often, this was done when the amount of the fee was reasonable and the master of the wrecked ship did not want to delay his voyage by going to Key West to testify in court. However, in accordance with the traditional rule of salvage, "no cure, no pay," if the wrecker failed to refloat the wrecked vessel, the agreement was off. When a ship loaded with ice ran ashore on American Shoals in 1856, the master did not wait long to agree to the wrecking captain's offer to haul him off for $1,500. Sometimes an agreement on salvage was made after the salvaged ship or cargo had been brought to Key West. The bark *Harriet and Martha* went ashore in the Dry Tortugas in 1854 and bilged. The wreckers brought part of her cargo of rice to Key West and agreed to accept sixty percent of the proceeds of the sale of the rice as salvage. Occasionally one side or the other would refuse to honor an agreement made on the reef, and the case would end up in court. The master of the brig *La Maria,* which ran ashore in the Dry Tortugas in 1838, claimed the wreckers had agreed to get him afloat for $400. Eight wrecking vessels manned by forty-five crewmen worked for fourteen days to get the brig off the reef. In court the wreckers denied that they had made any such deal and stated that the captain and crew of the brig were so worried they got down on their hands and knees and prayed. The judge, passing over the question of who was telling the truth, decreed a salvage award of $5,000 based on the work the wreckers had actually performed.

When the judge of the superior court was away or the master of the wrecked ship was in a hurry to resume his voyage, the master might agree to submit the claim to arbitration. But as a former Key West newspaper editor observed in 1833, "It may be set down as a rule, whenever during the presence of the Judge [of the superior court], a case is submitted to arbitration, foul play is intended." Another writer in 1842 advised, "*Never let your captains leave cases to arbitration on Key West;* for ten to one the persons selected will be part secret owners of the wrecking vessels to whom they are going to award the salvage; if not, then probably they have the supply of them, or they are otherwise too much interested to decide impartially." Commenting on the arbitrators' award in the case of the brig *Halcyon* (discussed more fully in Chapter 8), the lawyer Hackley wrote, "The case is palpably one of bribery, for as to Van Evour [one of the arbitrators], he has never had any character since I have known him and the wording of the award is sufficient to show what the principles of the others of necessity must be." Typically two men would be chosen as arbitrators. In the case of the brig *Mary Hart,* hauled off the reef by the wrecking sloop *Brilliant* in 1831, the two arbitrators gave an award more in line with what might have been decreed by the court. They valued the brig and cargo at $4,000 and awarded the *Brilliant* $1,000.

Unfortunately, there is very little information on how many claims were decided by agreement between the wrecked ship's master and the wreckers and how many were determined by arbitrators. Nor is it known how many times those involved resorted to arbitration because the judge was not in town. The largest number of settlements by arbitration, as far as is known, occurred in 1844, when fourteen of twenty-one salvage awards were made by arbitrators. But since these all took place consecutively over a period of four months, it is very likely that the judge was away. Based on an analysis of all available records, it does appear that the majority of salvage cases were adjudicated in court.

Everyone Was in on the Business

When a salvaged vessel or cargo arrived in Key West, the vessel's master would consign the vessel and cargo to one of the merchants to serve as his business agent. Being unfamiliar with the business community of Key West, the master would normally choose a merchant recommended by the wrecking captain in charge of the salvage operation. As was often the case, the merchant recommended would also be the owner or a part owner of the wrecking captain's vessel. For his services, the merchant received a commission on the value of the salvaged goods amounting to 5 percent on the first $5,000 dollars and 2.5 percent on the balance plus 1.5 percent on the cost of reshipping. If the cargo was perishable, the master would request a court order to allow its immediate sale.

If there was any question about the seaworthiness of the wrecked ship, the court would order a survey to determine whether it was fit to continue on its voyage, required repairs, or should be condemned and sold.

The arrival of a wrecked ship or salvaged cargo in Key West meant employment or profit for many people. Dockworkers offloaded cargo and stowed it in warehouses. The U.S. marshal accepted custody of the salvaged goods and ensured their security. Clerks marked and tallied cargo. Bookkeepers entered receipts and sales in ledgers. Surveyors assessed the seaworthiness of vessels that had been ashore and brought into port by the wreckers. Shipwrights, sailmakers, riggers, caulkers, blacksmiths, and other skilled craftsmen repaired damage. Ship chandlers supplied replacements of lost rigging, equipment, and provisions. Appraisers, appointed by the court, determined the value of the vessel and cargo saved. Proctors (lawyers) prepared libels (salvage claims) for the wreckers or responses (answers to the salvage claims) for the master, owner, and underwriters. Auctioneers sold the cargo after the judge's decision was handed down. In his diary, the lawyer Hackley commented, "Cargoes of wrecked vessels generally sell for their full value here or at least much better than anyone could suppose."

The merchants–and there were only four who owned wharves in 1839–stood to gain the most. If they owned one of the wreckers, they received half of the salvage award to that vessel in addition to a percentage on the value of the cargo consigned to them as business agent. They earned fees for mooring the salvaged vessel at their wharves, for offloading and hauling the cargo to their warehouses, and for storing and reloading cargo. If they purchased cargo at an auction, they normally made a profit on its resale. The outfitting, provisioning, upkeep, and repair of the wrecking craft were other major sources of income for Key West merchants, ship chandlers, and dockyards. In a letter to his relatives, a Key West lawyer wrote in 1838, "You will naturally enquire how we live, and the reply is very simple, in, by, and through wrecks–If we are not directly interested in the business, our support wholly comes from it. Stop that and we cease to live."

Differences of Opinion in the Wrecking Court

Generally, within a few days after the salvaged ship or cargo was brought to Key West, the wrecking captain's proctor would file his libel against the ship and cargo in court (unless the claim was submitted to arbitration). The libel included a narrative of the wrecking captain's version of events during the salvage operation. The proctor for the ship's master would file a response, which would contain the master's version of what transpired. Often differences between the two stories made the judge won-

American clipper ship *Eliza Mallory* went ashore north of Cape Florida in 1859 and was a total loss. Twelve wrecking vessels with 145 men, working from one to five weeks, saved entire cargo of cotton valued at $56,445. Ship's master complained wreckers were not very diligent in their work. (mezzotint, artist unknown. From the collections of The Mariners' Museum, Newport News, Virginia)

der if they were describing the same incident.

Almost always, the wrecking captain and the master of the wrecked vessel disagreed about the state of the weather. Whereas the wrecker might draw a picture of a howling gale with huge seas breaking across the decks, the master of the wrecked ship would describe conditions as a fresh breeze with a few whitecaps. In 1830, four fishing smacks went to the aid of a brig aground in the Dry Tortugas. Working in the midst of what they described as a "heavy blow," the smacks got the brig off. By the time they towed her into Tortugas harbor, they said it was blowing a "gale." In his response, the master of the brig observed that despite the "boisterous state of the weather, the libelants [fishing smacks] were not deterred from procuring a valuable fare of fish," and "as he is informed and believes and therefore avers, fishing can only be carried out during mild and calm weather."

In their efforts to get the judge to reduce the salvage award, masters of wrecked ships would often criticize or downplay the wreckers' work. Their favorite response was, "I could have gotten her off by myself, but decided to accept the wreckers' help because the weather might deteriorate." In 1842, thirty-eight men from three wrecking sloops worked for five hours offloading cargo from a brig aground on Carysfort Reef. Three times they carried out anchors and attempted to heave her off. On the third attempt, the brig came free, and the wreckers piloted her to Key West. In his response to the wrecker's libel, the brig's master claimed he could have gotten his ship off himself and accused the wreckers of delaying the process by taking the lighter cargo off first. The judge gave little credence to the master's claim and supported the wreckers' decision to take the lighter, more valuable cargo first on the chance that the ship might fill with water from a hole in her bottom.

Four wrecking sloops with forty-nine men worked for twenty hours offloading cargo, including kegs of gunpowder, from a brig wrecked on Great Conch Reef in 1843. In the heavy swell, two of the wrecking vessels were damaged while alongside. The wreckers brought the ship to Key West, where she was surveyed and found to be unworthy of repair. Despite these undisputed facts, the brig's master claimed there was not as much danger as the wreckers said, that there were more wrecking vessels and men than needed, and that the wreckers did not remove as much cargo as they said they did.

In other cases, masters of wrecked ships accused wreckers of being inexperienced, of having vessels that were too small, of failing to warn them of shoal water, of taking out more cargo than necessary, of pilfering cargo, of not exerting themselves sufficiently, and of getting drunk on the job. If any of the masters' charges were proven, and they usually were not, the judge would reduce the salvage award or, in serious cases of misconduct, take away the wrecker's license.

The judge of the superior court based the amount of salvage he awarded on the following considerations: the state of the weather and the willingness of the wreckers to go out in rough seas, the degree of risk of injury to the wreckers and to their vessels, the amount of labor and skill used in the operation, and finally, the value of the ship and cargo saved. Except in one unusual situation, there was no reward for saving lives. The judge tried to make the awards high enough to keep a sufficient number of wreckers working on the reef, but not so high as to encourage more than were nec-

Judge William Marvin, territorial and district judge of Superior and District Courts ("wrecking court") for twenty-two years: 1839 to 1845, 1847 to 1863 (courtesy of Monroe County Public Library)

essary or to make the work enormously profitable.

In his book *The Law of Wreck and Salvage,* Judge Marvin cites examples of amounts of salvage awarded in the cases of twenty-three wrecks that took place between 1823 and 1857. The average award was twenty-five percent of the value of the ship and cargo saved. The awards ranged from a low of three percent to a high of fifty percent, except a few cases in which the judge awarded sixty percent on cargo saved wholly by diving. The largest total salvage award was $47,971 for the cargo and materials saved from the ship *America,* lost on the Dry Tortugas in 1836.

An attorney who practiced in Key West for several years wrote in 1838:

> The whole mercantile business [in Key West] is done by three houses & two of these own vessels engaged in wrecking and the other is the friend, merchant, & banker of a person who owns a great interest in such vessels. Between

> these establishments, and the different societies engaged in wrecking, there is great competition. They watch each other with unsleeping eyes. Their charges are all the same. Each has a good wharff [sic] and warehouse, and, in this little secluded place, each knows the other's business, & if anything unfair should be done, it would soon be proclaimed. Others too are here, in the winter particularly, who are watching every movement of the residents, and who are ready to purchase on speculation, whenever an opportunity offers. There are three distinct interests and so great is the competition and watchfulness, that there is no fear that the business entrusted to either will not be fairly transacted.

But the Northern underwriters and insurance companies had quite a different view of what went on in Key West. They claimed that the merchants, by means of secret understandings, would agree not to drive up each other's bids when wrecked property was being sold at auction. They further claimed that auctions were deliberately held such a short time after the wrecked goods arrived in port that would-be bidders from out of town would not be able to get to Key West in time to bid against the local merchants, nor would the underwriters' agent be able to get there to pay salvage or purchase the goods if they had to be sold. An article in *Hunt's Merchants' Magazine,* written in 1842 by a journalist who claimed "a residence of a few years on the Florida reef," gave this view of an auction of wrecked property at Key West: "The day of sale arrives. Who are the bidders? The aforesaid five [Key West] merchants! How easily *might* these merchants agree not to run the one or the other on his bid, and thus a whole cargo, worth thirty thousand dollars, might be divided among them at the cost of about two thousand dollars each, or less. It is true, sometimes advertisements are sent to Havana; but sometimes also the sales take place before the merchants from there have a chance to get over to Key West, and *sometimes* this may be known when the advertisement is sent; but then the sending to Havana will have a good appearance when represented to underwriters and absent owners."

When Housman sought to have Indian Key designated a port of entry in 1838 and 1839, the underwriters supported his petitions, saying, "In addition to the facilities it would offer to save a greater amount of property, [an additional port of entry] would create competition with Key West, and be the means of preventing many of the gross frauds committed upon the underwriters." However, because of incorrect figures, distorted facts, and slanderous statements in the petitions, as pointed out in a memorial from William Whitehead of Key West, Congress declined to grant port of entry status to Indian Key.

The underwriters also suspected that some wrecking captains were making secret deals with the masters of wrecked ships to share the salvage awards in return for being allowed to be the exclusive salvagers. In one instance, an underwriter's agent obtained a sworn statement that proved such suspicions, and four wrecking captains lost their salvage awards as a result. Finally, around 1844, the underwriters recognized that they needed to have a representative on the scene and stationed a permanent agent in Key West to look after their interests.

Facts and Figures

The number of vessels wrecked and the number of wreckers in operation gradually increased with the increase in traffic through the Straits of Florida. In 1830, the *Savannah Georgian* reported that there were twelve or thirteen wrecking vessels manned by about 120 men. According to the *Key West Enquirer,* by November 1835 there were twenty full-time wrecking vessels plus a few smaller vessels that also had wrecking licenses. At the beginning of 1857, there were thirty-three licensed wrecking vessels having a total tonnage of 1,733 tons and carrying about 250 men. In 1858, there were forty-seven, half of which were fishing smacks. Judge Marvin considered this an adequate number and noted that the salvage awards were such that if a wrecker quit, there was always another ready to take his place.

The editor of *The Key West Gazette* in 1832 estimated that "the number of vessels wrecked on this coast amount to about ten or twelve per annum, probably averaging thirty thousand dollars each." In 1848, Stephen R. Mallory, collector of customs at Key West, wrote the superintendent of the coast survey, "The number of vessels publicly known to strike upon them [the reefs], including as well those extricated with or without the aid of wreckers, is not less than forty-eight per annum, or one in every seven days nearly; but it is confidently believed, from reliable sources of information possessed by the people of the coast, that many others strike upon the reefs and get off of which no accounts are published." That number gradually increased until it reached a peak in the 1850s. Court records, newspaper reports, and other sources show 248 wrecks between 1849 and 1859, but there were undoubtedly more that were not reported because the ship's crew got the vessel off or the master made a confidential agreement with the salvors. Salvage awards for the same period totaled $1.17 million, and this figure does not include awards made by direct negotiation or arbitration.

There are so many gaps and conflicts in the available data on wrecks and wrecking vessels that an accurate analysis of the profitability of the wrecking business on the Florida Reef is not possible. One source claims that by 1860, because of the income from wrecking, Key West was the richest city per capita in the United States. No facts are available to support this claim, but unquestionably, the residents of Key West, particularly the merchants who derived income from nearly every facet of the business, were prospering. One of those merchants, William Curry, who came to Key West from the Bahamas as a teenager and began work as an office boy, became Florida's first millionaire. Another measure of the income from wrecking is indicated by customs duties. Between 1823 and 1828, duties collected at Key West were ten times higher than those of all other Florida ports. Still, for the owners and crews of the vessels, wrecking was a highly speculative business.

Most salvage operations required the services of more than one wrecking vessel. The customary basis for dividing the salvage award among the vessels was "ton for ton and man for man." Half the total salvage award went to the vessels' owners divided according to the tonnage of their vessels. The other half went to the crews. The crew's half was divided in shares (as explained in Chapter 5). Thus, if there were two wreckers involved in a salvage operation, and one displaced one hundred tons while the other displaced fifty tons, the owner of the one-hundred-ton vessel would receive twice as much salvage money as the owner of the fifty-ton vessel.

Some idea of the odds against making a lot of money as an owner or crewman of a wrecking vessel can be seen in the wrecking data for the years

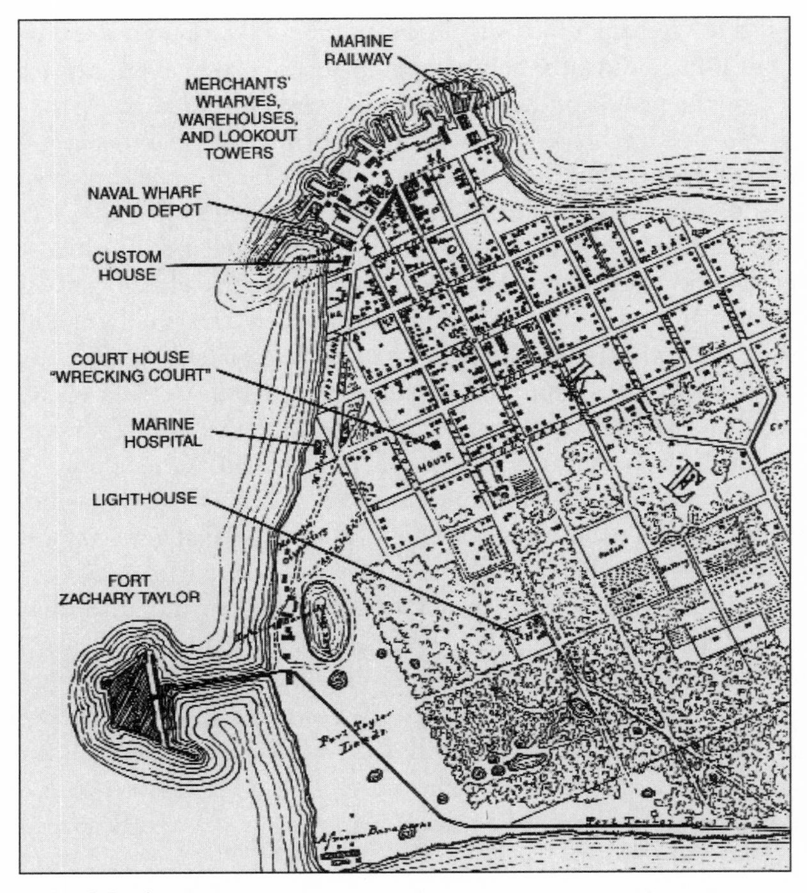

Key West in 1861 (Topographical Map of the Island of Key West. Compiled and drawn under the direction of Capt. E. B. Hunt, Corps of Engineers, by James C. Clapp, Draughtsman, Fort Taylor, September 1861. Courtesy of National Archives)

1835, 1848, and 1858. These years were selected because there is more complete data for them than for most other years. The admiralty court records for 1835 show that twenty-three vessels participated in salvaging one or more of sixteen wrecks. Only nine of these vessels salvaged more than one wreck, and six of the full-time wreckers did not manage to salvage even one wreck that year. Two wreckers worked on four wrecks each, and two more worked on only three.

The admiralty court records for 1848 show that thirty-eight vessels participated in salvaging one or more of twenty-one wrecks. The wrecking sloop *George Eldridge* worked on eight wrecks, but the sloop *Texas,* which worked on five wrecks, earned the most salvage money, approximately $10,800. However, more than half of the thirty-eight vessels worked on only one or two wrecks, and there were an unknown number that did not find any wrecks.

The owner of a typical wrecker had an investment of $2,500 in his vessel. A writer in 1840 estimated the annual expense to maintain and provision a typical wrecking vessel at approximately $2,700. Assuming these figures are correct, only six of the thirty-eight wrecking vessels finding wrecks in 1848 earned enough salvage to pay their owners' expenses. In 1858, only eight wrecking vessels out of forty earned enough to pay their owners' expenses. However, it should be remembered that wrecking was not the only occupation of many of the vessels. Some of them also served as pilot boats or were engaged in fishing, turtling, or carrying freight.

For the owners (other than merchant-owners) and crews, the wrecking business was a gamble. The owners wagered a substantial amount of money, and the crews wagered a great deal of time and risked death or injury. Experience and skill played an important role, but so did the luck of being in the right place at the right time when a ship drove up on the reef. In a memorial to Congress submitted in 1829, owners and captains of Keys wrecking vessels said, "We respectfully suggest that notwithstanding impressions abroad, there is no business, where the remuneration is so uncertain as that of wreckers, as it is not unusual for vessels to cruise a year without meeting any employment." Not many wrecking vessels or captains were successful enough to remain in the business for more than a few years.

Chapter 4

Wrecking schooner in heavy weather (*The Century Magazine,* Vol. XXXII, October 1886, No. 6, p. 817. From the collections of The Mariners' Museum, Newport News, Virginia)

WRECKING VESSELS

Types and Characteristics

The names of more than two hundred sailing craft displacing at least twenty tons, which engaged in wrecking at one time or another, appear in the wrecking court records between 1834 and 1861. Until the late 1850s, the majority were sloop-rigged, but by 1860 schooners outnumbered sloops almost two to one. The average tonnage and length of sloops remained steady at about fifty tons and sixty feet throughout the period, while average schooner size increased to about eighty tons and seventy feet in the 1850s.

In the early years, nearly all the wrecking vessels came from northern ports. In one month in 1830, the lawyer Hackley recorded in his diary the arrival of three sloops and one schooner for the purpose of becoming regular wrecking vessels. Two were from New York, one was from Connecticut, and one was from Baltimore. Of the twenty full-time wrecking vessels operating in the Keys in 1835, all except one were built in the North, principally in Maryland and Connecticut. Four of the wreckers were based at Indian Key, two at Key Vaca, and the remainder at Key West. Seven of the fourteen vessels based at Key West came from home ports in Connecticut, New

York, and Pennsylvania. In addition to these, a number of fishing smacks had wrecking licenses but engaged in wrecking only when the opportunity arose.

Desirable design characteristics for wrecking vessels included shallow draft (some had centerboards) to enable them to get alongside wrecks in shoal water, sharp lines with a generous spread of canvas for speed, and a large cargo storage capacity to take aboard as much of the wreck's cargo as possible. Some wreckers were former pilot, fishing, or cargo-carrying vessels adapted to the business, while others, particularly those built in Key West, were specifically designed for wrecking.

The largest sloop in the pre–Civil War period was the *Eliza Catherine,* originally built in New York in 1838. A hurricane drove her ashore on Key Vaca in 1846, where she landed in a settler's garden. After rebuilding in Key West, she measured 102 tons and 70 feet. In 1858, she was rerigged as a schooner. The next largest sloop, which remained a sloop throughout her career, was the ninety-six-ton, sixty-nine-foot *Texas.* Commanded by two of the most successful wrecking captains, she served as a wrecker for twenty-one years.

Until the late 1850s, the majority of wrecking vessels were sloop-rigged. (sloop *Moccasin,* built Key West 1888. Courtesy of the Historical Association of Southern Florida)

The largest schooner in the wrecking business was the Key West–built pilot boat *Florida,* which measured 171 tons and 90 feet and was valued at $8,000. Built in 1853, she aroused the envy of the other wreckers because of her great speed. During one race, she collided with the schooner *Dart,* doing considerable damage to her rival. Her brief career came to an end in 1857, when, as told in Chapter 6, she caught fire during a salvage operation and was destroyed.

John J. Audubon visited the Keys in 1832 and wrote the following description of a large wrecking schooner he went aboard: "As we approached the largest schooner, I admired her form, so well adapted to her occupation, her great breadth of beam, her light draught, the correctness of her waterline, the neatness of her painted sides, the smoothness of her well-greased masts, and the beauty of her rigging. . . . Silence and order prevailed on her decks. The commander and the second officer let us into a spacious cabin, well lighted and furnished with every convenience for fifteen or more passengers."

Another observer described the wrecking vessels he saw in 1857 as "the finest models I have ever seen for speed and for close sailing to the wind. They are built deep behind and barely resting on the water in front with raking masts and an enormous spread of canvas."

Salvage Equipment

To carry out salvage operations, wreckers needed special equipment such as heavy anchors, spare anchors, strong anchor chains, long hawsers, extra mooring lines, and large fenders. In 1852, the wrecking schooner *Lizzy Wall,* eighty tons, carried a 1,000-pound anchor and 70 fathoms (240 feet) of chain. In 1860, the relatively small wrecking schooner *J. H. Champlin,* 38 tons, had a 1,550-pound anchor.

Cargo handling operations required an extensive inventory of blocks, tackles, and line. Crewmen needed cotton hooks to handle the three-hundred- to five-hundred-pound cotton bales. Sometimes they had to cut through the deck or side of a wreck to get at the cargo, so a good supply of axes, saws, and other carpenters' tools was kept on board.

Around 1848, windmill-operated pumps became available in Key

Schooner *Raven*, built in Boston in 1836, typical of smaller New England–built wrecking schooners (watercolor by Mrs. A. Clive Edwards, courtesy of Peabody Essex Museum, Salem, Massachusetts)

West. Because they were large and cumbersome, they were not normally carried on board. When needed, wreckers would rent them, carry them to the scene, and set them up on the deck of the wreck. One such pump was reported to be capable of discharging about four thousand gallons per hour. Beginning about 1858, there was a steam pump in Key West, which could be hired along with an operator and transported out to a wreck to dewater it (remove the water) when manually operated pumps could not do the job.

The brig *Algerine* experimented with the use of a diving bell in the summer of 1835. With the bell on board, she sailed on a cruise along the reef. When she returned to port, the *Key West Enquirer* reported, "We regret that the enterprise of her [*Algerine*'s] proprietors has as yet been attended with little reward, but hope that enterprise will ultimately give them the success they merit." Apparently, the owners' enterprise was never rewarded, for there is no further mention of the use of a diving bell in newspapers or wrecking court records. One other instance of the use of special diving equipment occurred during salvage work on the wreck of the ship *Isaac Allerton,* sunk on Washerwoman Shoal in 1840. This was the largest salvage operation ever undertaken in the Keys. Divers recovered much of the cargo by free diving. Two or three months after the Keys wreckers had ceased operations, a schooner from Boston arrived on the scene equipped with "submarine armor" (presumably a diving suit and helmet) and brought up more cargo worth about a $1,000 dollars.

One or more heavy-duty boats were essential in wrecking operations. Wrecking captains needed them to board the wreck initially to assess the situation and to ask the master if he would accept assistance. Crewmen used them to take soundings around the wreck; to carry out anchors; to transfer mooring and towing lines; and, when the wrecking vessel could not get alongside the wreck because of shallow water, to transship cargo. The larger wreckers carried two boats called quarter boats on davits near the stern. Others carried a boat on davits at the stern or one or two nested on deck amidships. The boats could be sailed as well as rowed.

Some idea of the size of quarter boats is found in testimony from an 1848 wrecking case. Because of strong head winds, the sloops *Texas* and *Parallel* sent their quarter boats ahead to the wreck. Seven oarsmen manned one of the boats, and ten men rowed the other. According to the master of the wrecked ship, the "large" boat of the *Texas* had a keel length of fourteen feet and was able to carry out a one-thousand-pound anchor lashed to her stern.

One or more heavy-duty boats were absolutely essential to wrecking operations.
(*Harper's New Monthly Magazine,* July 1888. From the collections of The Mariners' Museum, Newport News, Virginia)

Part-time Wrecking Vessels

Just about every sailing vessel of any size operating in Keys waters had a wrecking license whether it was a fishing smack, sponge schooner, mail boat, or freight carrier. Pilot boats, whose principal function was to meet incoming ships and provide pilots to guide them into and out of Key West harbor, also carried wrecking licenses. Even full-time wreckers occasionally left the reef to transport salvaged goods to distant ports or to hunt turtles.

Fishing vessels, or smacks as they were called, were not well equipped to work as salvage vessels because they had small crews, usually five men, and limited cargo storage space because of the large live wells in which fish were stored. Nevertheless, they assisted in salvaging wrecks whenever the opportunity presented itself. The thirty-nine-ton, forty-two-foot, sloop-rigged smack *Morro Castle* generally spent her time fishing and carrying the live fish to the Havana market. But between 1835 and 1854, she also managed to participate in twenty-one salvage operations. Judge Marvin tried to discourage fishing vessels from acting as wreckers. In deciding a salvage case in 1843, he wrote, "In the present case, three out of five of the [salvage] vessels . . . were fishing smacks. It has often been cited in this court that they are not entitled to as high a reward as regular wreckers."

Much to the disgust of Key West residents waiting to hear from relatives up north, the mail boats did not hesitate to divert from their course when they saw a live turtle or a wreck on the reef. As late as 1887, a letter from Coconut Grove said, "My Dear Sisters: Owing to the wreck of a cotton ship in the Keys, the mail boats have paid more attention to delivery of cotton bales than to quick delivery of mail."

Sailing Craft Construction

The wrecking industry created a demand for shipwrights, caulkers, sailmakers, riggers, and other skilled craftsmen to maintain the wrecking vessels and to repair the salvaged vessels they brought back to port. Before long, these skilled workers turned their hands to building their own sailing vessels. The first recorded Key West–built vessel, the ten-ton sloop *Mary McIntosh* was launched in March 1835. The *Key West Enquirer* called her "a beautiful boat built on our own 'little isle.' She is said to be the first boat of

Sponge schooners such as these also engaged in wrecking when the opportunity presented itself. (courtesy of Monroe County Public Library)

her size which has been built here, being about 32 feet keel. The model is handsome and does honor to the gentlemen who built her. The builder is [sic] Mr. Curry and Mr. Bartlum."

William Curry, a merchant who later became Florida's first millionaire, was probably more involved in the financing than in the actual construction of the vessel. John Bartlum, a self-taught shipwright, came to Key West from Green Turtle Cay in the Bahamas. According to one biography, he never served a day as an apprentice but learned his skill from reading and practical application. The partnership between the two men continued, and when the firm of Bowne and Curry was organized in 1845, Bartlum was engaged as master shipwright. The first vessel he built for the firm, the *G. L. Bowne,* was a large schooner–120 tons, 77 feet in length–designed as a pilot boat and wrecker. According to lawyer William Hackley's diary, "She was built of native wood, principally wild tamarind with pitch pine planking, and laid on the building ways 'Conch' [Bahamian] fashion, bow out."

The launching of the *G. L. Bowne* in 1848 marked the beginning of a decade of building large sailing vessels that was never again equaled. Not surprisingly, it coincided with the peak years of the wrecking industry. In 1849, Bartlum built a 134-ton pilot-wrecking schooner, which was named *Euphemia* for Curry's wife. She proved to be such a fast-sailing vessel that a slave-trader purchased her in the expectation that she would be able to outrun the Navy's anti-slave patrol vessels. In his diary, Hackley recorded viewing another one of Bartlum's schooners in 1853. He wrote, "Saw the new pilot boat schooner which they have on the stocks. She is on the model of the Yacht *America* [which won the first America's Cup race in 1851], though a little larger and will be called *Young America*." In five years of service as a pilot boat before the Civil War, *Young America* salvaged eleven wrecks.

Between 1848 and 1860, Key West shipwrights built at least thirty wrecking vessels, ten of which displaced more than one hundred tons. Of these, Bartlum is known to have built at least five, among them the largest of all the wrecking schooners, the already-mentioned, ill-fated schooner *Florida.* Another, the 149-ton, 89-foot schooner *Gipsy,* visited Nassau in 1858. The local newspaper commented that she was "one of the most beautiful specimens of mechanism we have ever seen afloat in our harbor." Bartlum's crowning achievement was the construction in 1856 of the clipper ship *Stephen R. Mallory.* Named for Florida's U.S. senator from Key West who later became secretary of the Confederate Navy, the *Mallory* was 164 feet long and displaced 959 tons. She was the only clipper ship built in Florida or in the South by native craftsmen. Bartlum used native mahogany in her construction, and she came to be known as the "mahogany clipper," reportedly the only one in the world.

Because of the use of native woods, Keys-built vessels tended to last longer than their northern-built counterparts. The most important of the native woods was a type of mahogany called madeira by the Conchs, which once grew abundantly in the Keys. Madeira was a light, tough, long-lasting wood that was practically impervious to rot or teredo worms and was used principally for framing. Other native boat-building woods were Jamaican dogwood, mastic, and wild tamarind. A life of thirty years was not unusual for Keys-built vessels, and there are records of Keys sailing craft still in use fifty to eighty years after their construction.

Despite the long life of their hulls, few Keys wrecking vessels stayed in the wrecking business very long. It had nothing to do with their construction and everything to do with their success or lack of it in finding wrecks to salvage. Less than half of the 290 wrecking vessels whose names appear in pre–Civil War wrecking court records took part in salvage operations for

Construction and repair of sailing wreckers began in the 1830s and reached its peak in the 1850s. Key West led all other Florida ports in construction of sailing vessels until the end of the nineteenth century. (courtesy of Monroe County Public Library)

more than two years. Only fifteen vessels continued wrecking beyond ten years, and only one was still wrecking after twenty years. This was the sixty-nine-foot, ninety-six-ton sloop *Texas*. Under eleven different captains, between 1836 and 1860, the *Texas* salvaged at least eighty wrecks.

With the decline in wrecks after the Civil War, Key West shipwrights turned their talents from building wreckers to building smaller fishing, sponging, and freight-carrying sailing craft. Nevertheless, Key West led all other Florida seaports in the construction of sailing vessels through the remainder of the nineteenth century.

Chapter 5

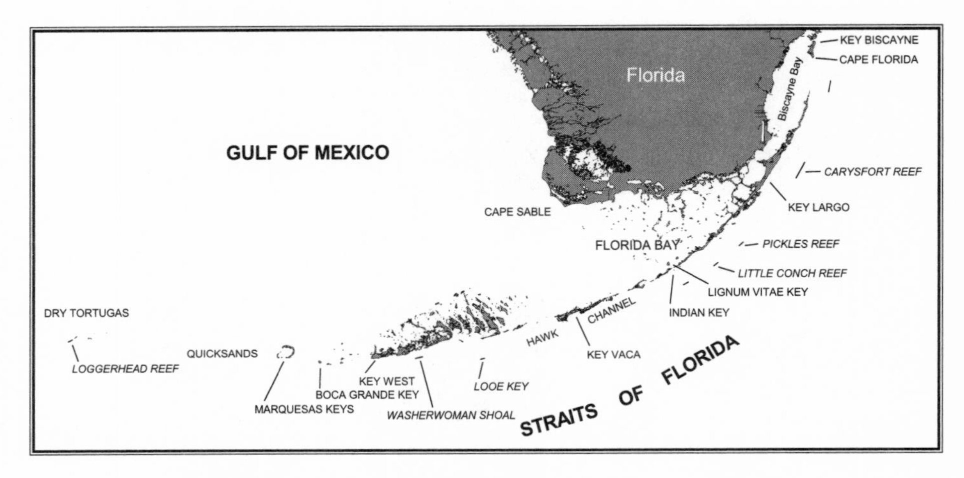

The Florida Keys and the Florida Reef (drawing by Erich Mueller)

WRECKING CREWS AND CAPTAINS

Crews—Rogues or Saviors?

"We are in the hands of the piratical wreckers!"—Captain of a ship wrecked in the Dry Tortugas in 1836.

"Well, I am here among the wreckers and pirates of Key West. . . . You have no idea how these people (a certain class called wreckers) mount at daybreak the lookouts, and if a sail is in the neighborhood of danger, how the vessels run out in storms and gales—such an energy, how admirable it would be, were it alone for charity and humanity, but alas! gain—gain! by the misfortunes of others is the sole impulse and all other feelings are strange to them."—F. H. Gerdes, U.S. Coast Survey, 1849.

"I was taught to believe that this class of men [wreckers] were an unprincipled set of beings who foraged on the misfortunes of others by plunder and depredation. On the contrary, I find them to be decent men of good common sense."—Letter from Key West by unknown correspondent, 1827.

> I am gratified with the opportunity of expressing on this as I have done on other occasions, my entire conviction that the course pursued by the individuals now engaged in this

> occupation [wrecking] on the coast of Florida, is as exemplary in regard to the rights of others, as that of any other class of this, or any other communities. They are the instruments of saving an immense amount of property, which without their exertions would be wholly lost, and so far as their conduct in rendering these services has come to the knowledge of this court (and it is often the subject of minute and critical examination), it has, with but few exceptions, been found correct, meritorious, and praiseworthy.
>
> –Judge Webb, judge of superior court, Key West 1838.

Where does the truth lie among these diverse views about the men who put out to sea in small sailing craft in the face of howling gales to save men, ships, and cargo cast up on the Florida Reef? There is no question that before the wrecking court was established in 1828, some of the wreckers engaged in shady dealings and dishonest practices. But a study of hundreds of wrecking cases after the court was in operation favors Judge Webb's view. The great majority of the wreckers were honest, hard-working men. But they were engaged in a dangerous and highly competitive occupation. Wrecking was a speculative business, and there was great pressure on the captains to make it profitable. There were many opportunities to take advantage of the helpless situation of a wrecked ship and its rich cargo, and now and then a captain or one of his crewmen would succumb to temptation.

While there were captains of wreckers who had their salvage awards reduced or lost their licenses because of misconduct, there is no documented instance in which a captain failed to put saving the lives of shipwrecked crews and passengers ahead of personal gain. A passenger from the ship *Amulet*, wrecked on the reef in 1831, had this to say of two wrecking captains: " . . . my most sincere thanks to Captains Smith and Place, commanding the sloops *Splendid* and *Hydes* [*Hyder*] *Ally*, for the kind and gentlemanly treatment I received from their hands whilst on board their vessels. Should it ever be my lot to be cast away again, I hope I may be fortunate enough to fall into the hands of those who have as much honor and fine feelings as the above-named captains."

Wrecking vessel crewman (courtesy of Florida State Archives)

Crew Size and Composition

Crew size varied depending on the size of the vessel and whether or not wrecking was its principal employment. A typical wrecking vessel carried a captain, mate, cook, six to eight seamen, and sometimes one or two young apprentices listed as boys. If a wrecker was in port when word of a wreck was received, the captain might sign on extra hands for that specific salvage job. Fishing smacks that also had wrecking licenses were manned by a captain and three or four hands. Captains often owned their vessels in full or in partnership with several other owners. Rarely did a wrecking vessel have the same captain throughout its life. For example, the schooner *Fair American* had nine captains from 1831 to 1840. Based on the 1840 census of Monroe County, there were 105 men engaged in wrecking at that time.

Next to the captain, the cook, usually a black man, was probably the most important man on board. Depending on his culinary skills, the crew was either a happy one or a disgruntled one. Another very important crew

Wrecking divers were often blacks.
(*Harper's Monthly Magazine*, Vol. 123, July 1911. Courtesy of Florida State Archives)

member was the diver. Most wreckers carried at least one diver, who was usually a black man. Working without benefit of any apparatus, wreck divers could free-dive to about seventy feet.

Most of the captains came from the New England or Middle Atlantic states or from the Bahamas. The seamen were of many different nationalities. A large number were Bahamians. One observer described the Bahamians, or Conchs, as they were termed, as long and lanky, tough and wiry, and capable of great endurance. They also had a number of sailors' superstitions. One was that if you slept on deck with the moonlight shining on your face, the moon's rays would draw the skin up so tight that you would not recognize yourself in a mirror the next morning.

A correspondent for the *Charleston Courier* sent this description of wrecking crewmen from Key West in 1854:

> The wreckers are a class *sui generus* [of their own kind]; they consist mostly of waifs on our shores from the maritime

> nations of the Old World; though most of the States of our Union have their representatives. Their language is equally heterogenous; each one has some pet word of his own engrafted upon the language in vogue. Their shares rarely exceed the ordinary wages of seamen; but influenced by the greater freedom from labor, and the hope of a prize, when once entered upon the business they seldom abandon it. Sometimes for a change they turtle or fish for a month or two, or squat down upon some Key with the intention of raising tropical fruits; but soon or late they are all at home again, on the forecastle of a wrecker. . . . They are noted generally for the facility with which they get rid of their money, and however a fat wreck may have filled their pockets, a week ashore will clean them out, and fit them for another cruise.

Dr. Benjamin Strobel, a physician and newspaper editor in Key West from 1829 to 1832, was on a voyage from Charleston to Key West in 1829 and was invited to be a passenger aboard a wrecking vessel. He wrote this impression of the crewmen he met:

> From all that I had heard of wreckers, I expected to see a parcel of low, dirty, pirate-looking crafts, officered and manned by a set of black-whiskered fellows, who carried murder in their very looks. I was, however very agreeably surprised, to find their vessels fine large schooners, regular clippers, kept in first rate order, and that the captains were jovial, good humored sons of Neptune, who manifested every disposition to be polite and hospitable, and to afford every facility to persons passing up and down the Reef. The crews were composed of hearty, well dressed honest looking men.

The wrecker Strobel was aboard, along with several others on their way to Key West, anchored in Bahia Honda harbor at four o'clock in the afternoon. Hunting parties went ashore, some to hunt deer and birds, others to search for shells. When the boats returned, the men took the game they had shot to the largest wrecker, where it was agreed that all the wrecking crewmen would gather for supper. Strobel described the evening this way:

> Our vessels were all lying within hail of each other, and as the moon rose, boats were seen passing from vessel to vessel, and all were busily and happily employed in exchanging courtesies and civilities. No one would ever have supposed, from the good feeling which appeared to prevail, that these men were professional rivals. About nine o'clock we started for supper; a number of persons had already collected. As soon as we arrived on board of the vessel, a German sailor, who performed remarkably well on the violin, was summoned to the quarter deck, where all hands, with a "good will and cheerily," danced to the lively airs which he played, until supper was ready. The table was laid in the cabin, and was literally loaded with venison, curlews, pigeons, and fish. Supper being ended, toasting and singing followed. Among other curious matters produced, I succeeded in preserving the following song, which was chanted by the fiddler who accompanied his voice with his instrument. The fiddler is the reputed author of the song. I shall make no apology for the poetry; it is certainly quite characteristic.

The Wrecker's Song

Come ye goot people von and all,
Come listen to my song,
A few remarks I have to make,
Which von't be very long.
Tis of a vessel stout and goot
As ever yet was built of woot,
Along de reef where de breakers roar,
De Wreckers on de Florida shore.
Chorus–Along de reef, etc.
The Tavernier's our rendezvous
At anchor dere we lie
And see de vessels in de Gulf [Straits of Florida]

Carelessly passing by;
When night comes on we dance and sing,
Whilst de current some vessel is floating in;
When daylight comes a ship's on shore,
Among de rocks where de breakers roar
    Along de reef, etc.
When daylight dawns den we're under veigh,
And every sail we set,
And if de wind it should prove light,
Why den our sails we'll vet;
To gain her first, each eager strives,
To save de cargo and de people's lives,
Amongst de rocks where de breakers roar,
De wreckers on de Florida shore.
    Along de reef, etc.
When we get 'longside we find she's pilged
[bilged],

Wreckers: rugged seamen who put out to sea in the face of howling gales to save men, ships, and cargo cast up on the Florida Reef (*Century Magazine*, July 1884. From the collections of The Mariners' Museum, Newport News, Virginia)

We know well what to do;
Save all de cargo dat we can,
De sails and de rigging too;
Den down to Key West we soon will go.
Where quickly our salvage we shall know,
When every ting is fairly sold,
Our money down to us it is told.
Along de reef, etc.
Den von week's cruise we'll have on shore
Pefore we do sail agen
And drink success to de sailor lads
Dat are ploughing of de main.
And when you're passing by dis way
On de Florida-reef should you chance to stray,
Why we will velcome you on shore,
Amongst de rocks where de breakers roar.
Along de reef, etc.

> The singer who had a broad German accent, laid great emphasis on his words. Between each verse he played a symphony, remarking–"I makes dat myself." The chorus was trolled by twenty or thirty hoarse voices, which in the stillness of the night, and at a little distance, produced no unpleasant effect.

Instead of being paid wages, the crew shared in the salvage awards. Half the salvage money went to the owner or owners and half to the crew. The crew's share was divided according to a standard rule. The captain received three shares, the mate two, the cook one and one-fourth, seamen one each, and boys one-half each. In vessels under thirty tons, the captain drew two shares, and in vessels under twelve tons, the captain and crewmen drew one share each.

In his book on the law of wreck and salvage, Judge Marvin cited a number of examples of salvage awards and resulting shares for crewmen. The average crew share for the eighteen wrecks he discussed was $83. The highest share, with the exception of divers, was $188. This was the amount received by thirty-nine crewmen from three wrecking vessels for salvaging the ship *Mississippi*, ashore on Looe Key in 1840. Working without rest from four o'clock in the afternoon until six o'clock the next morning, the crewmen offloaded thirty tons of cargo, threw over sixty tons of stone ballast, and heaved the vessel afloat.

The crewmen of the sloop *Mystic* received much lower shares for salvaging the ship *James* in 1836. The four seamen received $14.90 each. The captain, who was also a part owner, received three shares plus one-eighth of the owners' share for a total of $62.35. Shares in other salvage cases might be as low as $1, or, if neither the ship nor the cargo was saved, nothing.

Divers, particularly when they had to swim down into the foul water of a fully-submerged cargo hold, received higher shares than anyone else. The ship *Isaac Allerton* drove over the reef and sank in thirty feet of water on Washerwoman Shoal in 1856. Divers swam into the hold and attached lines to the cargo containers mostly by feel. One diver was awarded $769; six other divers received $500 each. On the other hand, the four hundred non-divers, who worked on the wreck over a period of six weeks, received only $50 each on average.

Captain Cole, retired wrecking captain, lived on Lignumvitae Key and grew watermelons in 1870s. (*Harper's New Monthly Magazine,* Vol. XLII, Dec. 1870–May 1871, courtesy of Monroe County Public Library)

Wrecking Captains

Analysis of pre–Civil War wrecking court records shows that not many captains salvaged enough wrecks to stay in the business for more than a few years. Of the 368 captains whose names appear in court records before the Civil War, it appears that more than half gave up wrecking after one or two years. Of the remainder, more than 80 percent quit after five or fewer years, and less than 5 percent continued wrecking for more than ten years.

The names of three pre–Civil War captains stand out above all the rest. Based on the available wrecking court records, John H. Geiger, William H. Bethel, and Richard Roberts spent more years as wreckers and salvaged more wrecks than any other captains.

John H. Geiger

As the wind increased to gale force and anchors began to drag, the wrecking vessels, one by one, gave up and ran for shelter in Key West harbor. Finally, only the schooner *Champion,* with Capt. John H. Geiger in command, remained standing by the wreck on Washerwoman Shoal. When the wind moderated the next day, the six wreckers who had fled to port returned to find the *Champion,* now alongside the wreck, hard at work offloading cargo.

Such dogged determination in the midst of adverse conditions was typical of Captain Geiger. A man who knew him well, William Marvin, the judge of the superior court at Key West, said, "Mr. John Geiger was pilot, captain of a wrecking vessel, a man of decided character, and a sort of commodore among his compeers."

Born in St. Augustine in 1807, Geiger became familiar with Keys waters as a young man. In 1823, while still in his teens, he became a pilot for Commodore Porter's antipiracy squadron. After Porter left Key West in 1824, Geiger remained as a harbor pilot, the first to be licensed in the territory, and also began to engage in wrecking. Information about some of his wrecking exploits is contained in fifty-seven wrecking court cases between 1835 and 1876. These are only a portion of the total he was involved in, but they amply demonstrate his skill as a seaman and a salvager. During the forty-one years that these wrecking court cases cover, Geiger captained eleven different vessels.

Capt. John H. Geiger, "a man of decided character and a sort of commodore among his compeers" (*Harper's New Monthly Magazine*, April 1871, "Along the Florida Reef," by Dr. J. B. Holder, courtesy of Monroe County Public Library)

He was also the owner or part owner of twelve wrecking vessels.

There are no records of Geiger's wrecking activities before 1835. In that year, at different times, he commanded two wrecking schooners, the ninety-four-ton *Caroline* and the forty-three-ton *Hester Ann.* The following year, Geiger became part owner and captain of the forty-four-ton sloop *Citizen.* In a period of just three months, he participated in five salvage operations. One of these was the wreck of the ship *America,* a total loss on Loggerhead Reef in the Dry Tortugas. Geiger shared in the salvage award of $47,971, the largest amount awarded up to that time. Shares for crewmen averaged $150 each.

Between 1835 and 1845, Geiger became the owner or part owner of six wrecking vessels and commanded three of them. By 1845, he had accumulated enough capital to purchase a pilot-wrecking schooner built to his order in Baltimore. Named *Louisa* after his first child, she displaced fifty-four tons and was sixty-one feet in length. In October 1845, a hurricane drove the *Louisa* out of Key West harbor and across the reef, where she sank in forty-two feet of water. As reported in the *Key West Gazette,* "On the very brink of the bottomless Gulf Stream, [the *Louisa*] was rescued only by the perseverance and skill of her owner, has undergone a complete and thorough repair, and is now in fact a new vessel." Just two months after she sank, Geiger raced the *Louisa* against the *Lafayette,* a schooner of comparable size, to a wreck some fifteen miles from Key West. The *Louisa* won by five miles.

Almost exactly one year later, on October 11, 1846, another hurricane, the worst ever to strike Key West, passed through the Keys. Nearly all the wrecking vessels on the reef were sunk, dismasted, or washed high and dry on shore. The *Lafayette* went down with all hands. The *Louisa* sank in Key West harbor, but her crew was saved. Undaunted, Geiger raised the *Louisa* a second time, refitted her, and resumed piloting and wrecking.

Three years later, in 1849, Geiger became captain of the newly launched, Baltimore-built pilot schooner *Champion.* At ninety tons and seventy-three feet, the new schooner proved to be a real champion for Geiger. Whether she was built to his order is not known, but a certificate of enrollment shows he was her owner as well as captain in 1851. Geiger and the *Champion* guided vessels in and out of Key West harbor and salvaged

Captain Geiger's home today, now called the Audubon House (photo by the author)

wrecks along the reef for fourteen years. Court records for that period show that Geiger and *Champion* were involved in thirty-seven salvage operations, but there were undoubtedly more.

At the same time, Geiger's family was growing. By 1849, his wife of twenty years, Lucretia Saunders, had delivered eight daughters and three sons. Three of their children died in childhood. Theirs was the largest family in the town. According to Jefferson Browne, a contemporary, Geiger's home "which stands on the corner of Whitehead and Greene Streets was for many years the center of a joyous social life."

An incident involving Geiger and the *Champion* in 1853 illustrates how competitive the wrecking business was. A British brig had gone ashore on Boca Grande Key, about twelve miles west of Key West. At the time the news reached Key West, the wind was light, so several wrecking captains set out in oared boats in a race to be the first on board the wreck. Their respective wrecking vessels, under the command of the mates, also got under way to follow them. Christopher Dunn, who was temporarily in command of the *Champion,* and one other captain headed out in a ten-oared boat. They had rowed about a mile from Key West when a twelve-oared boat carrying six captains got under way, passed them, and reached the wreck first. By an accepted rule of wrecking, the first captain to arrive at a wreck became the wreck master and was in charge of all subsequent salvage operations. When the *Champion* arrived at the scene, the wreck master refused to allow her to work the wreck. Geiger petitioned the court for a share in the salvage award on the basis that the *Champion* had been improperly excluded from participating in the salvage. He claimed that although the *Champion's* acting captain was one of the last to board the wreck, the vessel herself was the fourth to arrive on the scene. According to another wrecking rule, wreckers were to be admitted to participate in a salvage operation in the order in which the vessels, not the captains, arrived on the scene. Judge Marvin agreed and awarded the *Champion* a share in the salvage decree.

It appears that Geiger ceased salvage operations as a regular occupation sometime after 1862 but continued piloting. A document signed in 1865 certifies Captain Geiger, master of the schooner *Champion,* as a full branch pilot for the reef and harbor of Key West. Three years later he became owner and captain of a smaller vessel, the thirty-five-ton, sixty-five-foot pilot schooner *Nonpariel.* In this schooner, according to Jefferson Browne, Geiger "claimed to have beaten up Nassau harbor under jib alone to show the Conchs what an American vessel can do." As far as is known, he participated in only one salvage operation with the *Nonpariel.* In 1876, when he was seventy, his crew, along with the crews of twenty-two other wrecking vessels, assisted in offloading the steamship *City of Houston,* which had gone ashore off Saddle Hill Key, about fifteen miles to the east of Key West. Four years later, probably because of declining fortunes and health, he sold the *Nonpariel* and cast his anchor ashore.

With his income from wrecking and piloting gone, and for other unknown reasons, Geiger's once-considerable wealth melted away, and he was forced to sell a portion of his property to maintain his home and family. Described as "Dutch built, portly, large blue eyes, and thin white hair," he spent his final years up in the cupola of his house–which still stands at the corner of Whitehead and Greene Streets–with a spyglass, observing the passing ships. A superb seaman and acknowledged leader among the wreckers of the Florida Reef, Captain Geiger died in 1885 at age seventy-eight.

William H. Bethel

The son of a Bahamian wrecking captain, William Henry Bethel came to Key West with his parents in 1825. Under his father's guiding hand, he became a skilled seaman and, by 1832, a wrecking captain in his own right. He married a fellow Bahamian, Caroline Mott, in 1832. The following year, Caroline delivered the first of their seven children. Around 1834 or 1835, both Bethel families moved to Key Vaca to join the newly formed Bahamian settlement there. The younger Bethel quickly became one of the community's leaders. In 1836, he was appointed inspector of elections and, in 1840, justice of the peace.

In partnership with William Whitehead, another Key Vaca community leader, Bethel was part owner of a small, thirteen-ton, freight-carrying and wrecking schooner, the *Charlotte,* in 1834. The earliest record of his salvage operations is contained in the wrecking court records of that same year, when, at age twenty-five, he was captain of the thirty-eight-ton, fifty-one-foot schooner *Single Sailor.* Bethel purchased another small schooner, the fifteen-ton *Mary,* in 1835. This may have been the same *Mary* that was attacked and destroyed by Seminole warriors at Key Tavernier in October 1836.

About this same time, again in partnership with Whitehead, Bethel invested in a much larger wrecker, the sixty-four-ton, sixty-two-foot sloop *Ludlow.* Serving as her captain from 1836 to 1839, he salvaged many wrecks, twelve of which he libeled in superior court.

One of the wrecks was the bark *Rosalind,* ashore on Pickles Reef in July 1837. Part of the cargo was rum in kegs. When the wrecking vessels could not get alongside because of the heavy seas, Bethel, with his usual resourcefulness, directed the wrecking crewmen to heave the rum kegs overboard. The kegs floated over the reef into the calmer waters of Hawk Channel, where the wreckers' boat crews recovered them without difficulty.

Bethel was one of a number of wrecking captains from Key Vaca and Key West who signed a memorial to Congress in 1839 against allowing Indian Key to become a port of entry. He then drew up a petition to make Key Vaca a port of entry. Congress rejected both the Indian Key and Key Vaca petitions, and Key West remained the only port south of St. Augustine where salvaged cargoes from foreign ports could be entered through customs.

During the late 1830s, Dr. Henry Perrine, a physician and noted horticulturist temporarily residing on Indian Key, visited Key Vaca periodically to treat the sick and injured settlers and to encourage them to experiment with commercial crops such as sisal and cotton. One of his seriously ill patients was Bethel, who afterwards credited Perrine with saving his life.

In August 1840, a large band of Seminole Indians attacked and destroyed the wrecking settlement on Indian Key. The Bethels suffered a double loss from the raid. During the course of the attack, warriors killed Dr. Perrine, Bethel's friend and savior, and John Mott, his wife's brother. According to a newspaper report of the time, after receiving news of the attack, most of the settlers on Key Vaca fled to Key West. It is probable that the Bethels were among them. In any event, by 1850 the Bethel family was living in Key West.

Bethel's longest wrecking command was the ninety-six-ton sloop *Texas.* He became her captain in 1839 and remained as such for the next sixteen years, a longer time in continuous command of the same wrecking vessel than any other pre–Civil War captain. In the wrecking court records, there is testimony on forty salvage operations conducted by Bethel while he was captain of the *Texas.* Undoubtedly, there were more that were settled by negotiation or arbitration.

Bethel gave up command of the *Texas* in 1854 and, sometime between 1850 and 1856, moved his family to Indian Key. In May 1856, during the Third Seminole War, he wrote a letter to the owner of Indian Key advising that he had reports of Indians moving through the Keys. Although there were a number of houses on the key, there was only one other man besides Bethel to defend the place against an attack. In response to the owner's plea, the Army stationed a small detachment of soldiers to protect the settlers but in the fall of the following year reduced it to just four men. Bethel wrote the colonel commanding Army forces in Florida asking him to increase the force "sufficiently to mount guard during the night." But the Seminoles did not come to the Keys and by the end of the year had given up their fight.

According to the 1860 census, Bethel was "inspector of [election] returns" at Indian Key. The 1870 census lists him as a farmer, but he certainly had not given up the sea or wrecking. In 1861, he was captain of the wrecking schooner *Lavinia.* Between 1863 and 1870, he was captain of three different schooners and one sloop in addition to being owner and captain of the ten-ton schooner *Manatee* and the five-ton schooner-boat *Indian Hunter.* During these closing years of his wrecking career, he took part in eight salvage operations that there are records of.

In two salvage operations that are unique in wrecking court annals, Bethel served as wreck master but did not command a wrecking vessel. The first of these took place in 1863. One evening in March, two men in a boat from the Carysfort Lighthouse landed at Indian Key and informed Bethel that a bark was ashore about twelve miles from the lighthouse. Bethel's own boat, the *Indian Hunter,* was not available so he went with the men in their boat back to the lighthouse. After disembarking the keepers, he sailed the lighthouse boat to the wreck, arriving at four o'clock in the morning. When regular wrecking vessels arrived on the scene at daybreak, they accepted Bethel as wreck master. Had it been anyone else but Bethel, it is doubtful they would have done so.

The second incident occurred in October 1863. The day after a hurricane, Bethel sighted from his house the hull of a wrecked vessel about a mile

The day after a hurricane in October 1863, Bethel sighted from his house a wrecked ship about one and a half miles from Indian Key. (*Illustrated London News*, Vol. 19, Oct. 17, 1896, p. 505. From the collections of The Mariners' Museum, Newport News, Virginia)

and a half southwest of Indian Key. All the wrecking vessels in the area had been driven ashore, and their crews were in the process of trying to haul them off. Bethel, accompanied by several other men, rowed to the wreck in a small boat and offered his services to the wrecked ship's master. He then returned to Indian Key, informed the captain of the largest wrecker, still trying to get his vessel afloat, of the situation, and returned to the wreck. In the meantime, the crew of a small schooner had gotten their vessel afloat and were alongside the wreck offloading cargo. Bethel remained on board the wreck, directing operations as more wreckers arrived. Despite the fact that he did not command a wrecking vessel, he shared in the salvage award.

Bethel's last known salvage operation took place in 1870, when he was sixty-one years old. As captain of the schooner *Antonio,* he assisted in salvaging a cargo of sugar from the bark *Star,* ashore and bilged on Little Conch Reef.

In 1876, Bethel welcomed an unexpected visitor, Henry E. Perrine, son of Dr. Perrine and a survivor of the Seminole warriors' raid on Indian Key thirty-six years earlier. In an account of his return to Indian Key, Henry wrote that he had met "old Captain Bethel" and described him as a "kind-hearted old gentleman" who had a watermelon patch and pineapples growing on nearby Lignumvitae Key.

According to the 1880 census, Bethel, at age seventy, was still living on Indian Key with his wife. There is no record of his death, but it is likely that he died there, still searching the horizon for the sight of another wreck on the reef.

Richard Roberts

A Bahamian, a Southern sympathizer, and a self-professed man of religion, Capt. Richard Roberts began wrecking in the Keys long before he became a U.S. citizen. The earliest record of his salvage operations is in an 1829 wrecking court case, at which time he was a resident and citizen of the Bahamas. The judge of the superior court at Key West awarded him thirty percent of the net proceeds of the sale of a brig and cargo he had saved. Although the 1825 act of Congress was designed to exclude Bahamian wreckers from the Keys, it did not forbid them from operating there provided they brought the ships and cargoes they salvaged to a U.S. port of entry.

Capt. Richard Roberts (*Kinfolks*, Vol. II, by William Curry Harllee, New Orleans, 1934, courtesy of Monroe County Public Library)

For the next eleven years, while still a citizen of the Bahamas, Roberts conducted salvage operations in the Keys as captain of five different wrecking vessels. In the late 1830s, he salvaged at least a dozen ships as captain of the *Texas*. Near the end of 1839, he turned over command of the *Texas* to William Bethel and took over as captain of the ninety-four-ton, seventy-one-foot sloop *Key West*.

Throughout this period, Roberts continued to return to his home in the Bahamas between wrecking voyages. In 1834, at age thirty, he married seventeen-year-old Amelia Curry of Green Turtle Cay. The couple's first two sons, born in the Bahamas, died in infancy. The loss of their newborn children was to be a continuing source of grief for Richard and Amelia and perhaps had something to do with their decision to move to Key West. In 1838, Roberts purchased property in Key West, and, in 1840, the Roberts family moved to their new home and applied for U.S. citizenship.

In the continuing struggle between the slave owners in the South and the abolitionists in the North, Roberts' sympathies were with the Southerners. By 1844, Roberts had left the *Key West* and was captain of the eighty-eight-ton sloop *Eliza Catherine*. On an early July morning of that year, while cruising along the reef off Key Largo, *Eliza Catherine*'s lookout sighted a small sloop. Roberts took up chase and soon came up alongside an open boat occupied by one white man and seven black men. Suspecting the black men were runaway slaves and knowing there would be a reward for their return, Roberts took all the men into custody. Roberts' suspicions proved correct. The white man was Jonathan Walker, a Northern abolitionist who had taken the slaves aboard in Pensacola and was helping them to escape to freedom in the Bahamas. Roberts carried Walker and the slaves to Key West, where they were briefly imprisoned before being transported back to Pensacola.

In November, Roberts sailed to Pensacola to testify against Walker at his trial for slave stealing. The jury found Walker guilty, and the judge sentenced him to be pilloried, branded on the hand with the letters "S.S." for slave stealer, and fined. After the sentence was carried out, Walker was returned to prison, where he remained for almost a year until Northern abolitionists were able to pay his fine and court costs. Walker's branding aroused heated passions among the abolitionists and was the subject of an inflammatory poem, "The Branded Hand," written by John Greenleaf Whittier.

After his return to freedom, Walker wrote his recollections of his capture, trial, branding, and imprisonment. Of Roberts he had this to say: "Captain Roberts manifested great seriousness and devotion to the cause of religion. Yet profanity passed freely in the cabin and about his vessel's decks unrebuked. And I could not but think that he did not pay any too strict regard for honesty, as several articles that were taken from my boat on board of his vessel, could not be found by the sheriff, who went on board for them. I tried to have some conversation with him while on board, but that he carefully avoided by keeping at a distance."

After relinquishing command of the *Eliza Catherine* in 1848, Roberts became captain of one of the largest wrecking vessels on the reef, the 120-ton, 77-foot schooner *George L. Bowne,* built in Key West by John Bartlum. While in command of the *Bowne*, he saved a ship that had been given up for lost by the first wreckers to arrive on the scene.

The ship *William Hitchcock* had gone ashore in the Dry Tortugas in January 1849. The first group of wreckers had found her full of water and, believing the ship's hull was stove in, had stripped her of her rigging, furnishings, and a few bales of hay. The shipping agent in Key West asked Roberts to go to the Tortugas and inspect the condition of the ship to see if there was any possibility of saving her.

Upon reaching the scene in company with another wrecker, the schooner *William Chestnut,* Roberts' divers reported that the *Hitchcock's* hull appeared intact. Roberts sent the *William Chestnut* back to Key West to bring out a windmill pump. The windmill, pumping at 4,140 gallons per hour, lowered the water level in the hold to three feet overnight. At this point, Roberts' divers discovered that ten holes had been drilled through the hull with an auger in an apparent attempt to make the ship remain a total loss. The divers plugged the holes while other crewmen put back some of the ballast they had offloaded. After four days of carrying out anchors and heaving on the anchor lines with the capstan, the wreckers got the ship afloat, rerigged her, and sailed her to Key West. In all, twenty-eight crewmen from the *Bowne* and the *Chestnut* worked eighteen days to save the ship. Judge Marvin decreed a salvage award of $5,148, which resulted in shares of $117 for the vessels' crewmen.

Roberts left the *Bowne* in 1853 and served as captain of seven different wreckers between 1854 and 1860. In command of the *Texas* once again in 1858, he suffered a reprimand from Judge Marvin. While searching for wrecks along Carysfort Reef in May of that year, Roberts discovered a ship aground on Elbow Reef. Assisted by eleven other wrecking vessels that arrived on the scene at various times, Roberts directed offloading and carrying out anchors. After three days of offloading, the wreckers heaved the ship afloat only to find their way blocked by another shoal. A day and a night passed before the wrecking crewmen finally kedged the ship clear of the shoals. In court, the ship's master accused Roberts of mishandling the salvage operation. Judge Marvin agreed. Saying that Roberts erred in not taking more complete soundings, the judge reduced the salvage award from $23,000 to $18,000.

Having given birth to eleven children, six of whom died in infancy, Amelia Roberts died in 1856 at age thirty-nine. Soon thereafter, the grieving Roberts moved his family to Manatee County (just south of Tampa). The 1860 census listed his occupation as "farmer," but wrecking court records show that he was still involved in wrecking in the Keys up to May 1862.

A little over a year later, in August 1863, Roberts and two other men were sailing in a small open boat near Punta Rassa. They sighted a sloop that they suspected was a Union naval vessel and sailed into a creek to hide. An officer on the sloop saw Roberts' boat, rowed into the creek, and surprised the three men. In an ironic reversal of fates, Roberts suddenly found himself in remarkably similar circumstances to those faced by abolitionist Jonathan Walker nineteen years earlier. The Union naval officer placed Roberts and his two companions under arrest as blockade runners. Although there was no contraband in the boat, a witness testified that Roberts had refused to take an oath of allegiance to the United States. According to one of his descendants, Roberts had indeed become a blockade runner for the Confederacy and was engaged in carrying men from occupied towns to join the Confederate Army, as well as transporting much-needed provisions and supplies for the rebel troops. Roberts was taken to Key West as a prisoner and later paroled.

Roberts remained in Key West, living with his two sons. At the end of the Civil War, he resumed his wrecking career. It also appears that he engaged in other maritime pursuits. He was captain of a fishing smack in 1867 and was listed as a pilot in the 1870 census. He conducted his last known salvage operation in 1872, at age sixty-eight, as captain of a small six-ton schooner named *Gipsey*.

Based on available wrecking court records, Richard Roberts commanded more wrecking vessels–a total of sixteen over a period of forty years–and salvaged more wrecks than any other pre–Civil War captain. Six years after his last known salvage operation, he died in Key West at age seventy-four.

Chapter 6

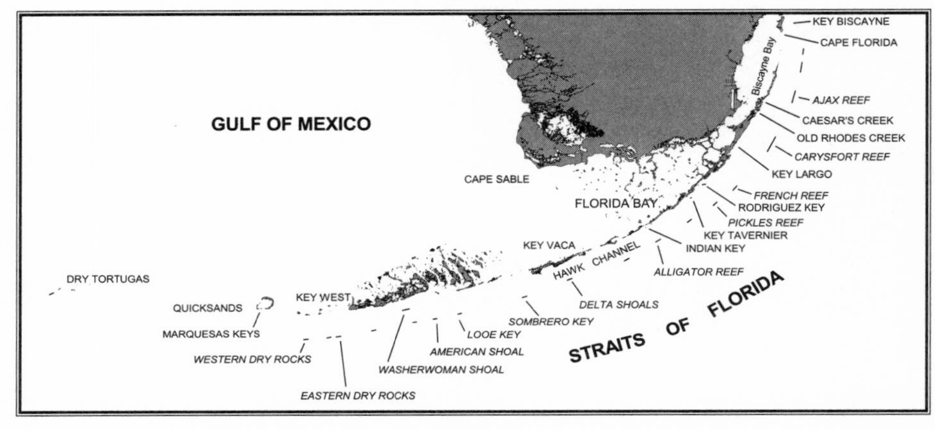

The Florida Keys and the Florida Reef (drawing by Erich Mueller)

SALVAGE OPERATIONS

Wrecking Legends

Romanticized stories of Florida Keys wrecking begin with the cry "Wreck ashore!" followed by scenes of seamen dashing to the waterfront to board their vessels for a race to the site of the wreck. The fact is, Keys wreckers did not sit around in port waiting to hear news of a wreck ashore. They spent most of their time on station in areas where the incidence of wrecks was high. According to wrecking court records from 1828 to 1861, eighty-five percent of all wrecks were discovered by wrecking vessels while cruising or at anchor along the reef.

How often the cry "Wreck ashore!" was heard in Key West is debatable. If first news of a wreck was brought to Key West by a passing ship, and particularly if the wreck was a large ship requiring many wreckers to offload it, then the news would quickly circulate around town. But this was seldom the situation.

It is also true that there were lookout towers over merchants' warehouses, but few wrecks occurred within sight of Key West. In fact, out of 315 wreck sightings in pre–Civil War admiralty court records, only 3

"Wreck ashore!" A romanticized view of wrecking in the Florida Keys (drawing by Kathleen Elgin. Courtesy of Oldest House and Wreckers Museum, Key West, Florida)

were sighted from Key West. The towers were built as much for sighting incoming vessels in order to prepare to receive them or to send a boat to meet them as for sighting wrecks on the reef. The arriving vessel might bring word of sighting a wreck up the reef or it might be a vessel that had been wrecked and was in need of repairs. It is also difficult to believe that a lookout sighting a wreck off Key West would run around town broadcasting the news. It is much more likely that he would quietly pass the information to his boss, a merchant and presumably the owner of several wrecking vessels, one of which might be ready to get under way and be the first to the wreck.

Another untrue wrecking legend is the story of unscrupulous men hoping to cause a wreck by placing false lights on shore. This simply wasn't done because it wouldn't work. Mariners are not *attracted* to lights. Quite the contrary, the sight of a light warns them that they may be standing into danger. Furthermore, for lights to be seen any distance at sea in the era of oil lanterns, they had to be specially designed and constructed, great in size and candlepower, operated by complex mechanisms, and mounted at considerable height. In all the wrecking court cases, there is no instance in which the master of a wrecked ship alleged that he was led aground by a false light. The master of the ship *Diadem*, which went ashore on Looe Key in 1856, claimed that he saw a bright flashing light, which he thought was Sand Key. As a result, he changed course and went aground. He did not claim it was a false light, merely that he was unable to account for it. It might have been a natural phenomenon, such as distant lightning, or a desperate attempt on the master's part to excuse running his ship aground.

Patrol Stations and Searches

After loading enough provisions and stores (paid for by the owner) for several weeks, a wrecking vessel would proceed to an area of the reef where the chances of finding a wreck were high. The greatest number of wrecks occurred in the upper Keys, particularly on Carysfort Reef, French Reef, Pickles Reef, and Alligator Reef. The next highest number of wrecks took place in the Dry Tortugas area. The reefs off the lower Keys were next in order, with most of the unfortunate ships grounding on American Shoals and Looe Key. The middle Keys area attracted wrecks to Delta Shoal and Sombrero Key. Other high-incidence wreck areas were the Eastern and Western Dry Rocks off Key West, the Quicksands to the west of the Marquesas Keys, and the reefs to the south of Cape Florida at the southern tip of Key Biscayne. Keys wreckers also went to the aid of vessels ashore on the mainland coast as far north as Hillsboro Inlet.

In the upper Keys, wreckers mostly used the anchorages at Indian Key, Key Tavernier, Rodriguez Key, and Caesar's Creek. At first light each morning, the wreckers would get under way from their anchorage to search along the reef. To ensure that no one had an unfair advantage, it was the custom for all to weigh anchor at the same moment. If there were several wreckers in the same area, by mutual agreement each wrecker would search a designated sector of the reef. When two wreckers converging on opposite courses sighted each other, they would know they had completed a full sweep of their sectors and would return to anchor, usually by ten o'clock in the morning. The crew would spend the rest of the day at various maintenance tasks such as resetting and tarring the standing rigging or scraping and slushing down (greasing) the masts. They would often go ashore to cut stovewood, get water, or hunt deer. For amusement and relief from the heat, they would put a sail in the water suspended so as to form a pool and bathe in it. When several wrecking vessels were anchored in the same harbor, the men would visit back and forth by boat. In the evening, they might all gather on one of the larger vessels for a night of feasting, singing, and dancing.

Even while at anchor, wreckers maintained a sharp lookout both day and night. In the middle of the night, a lookout on the wrecking sloop *America*, anchored off Key Largo, sighted a light on the reef. The *America* and another wrecking sloop, the *Mount Vernon*, got under way immediately, but the light went out. Instead of returning to harbor, the wreckers anchored in the lee of the reef. At first light, they discovered the source of the light, a brig ashore on French Reef. An even more alert lookout was on watch on board the sloop *Randall H. Greene*, anchored at Rodriguez Key. At two-thir-

Wrecking schooner racing to a wreck on the reef at night (*Harper's Weekly,* Vol. 3, April 21, 1860. From the collections of The Mariners' Museum, Newport News, Virginia)

ty in the morning, the lookout saw, through his spyglass, the dim silhouette of what might be a vessel on the reef. Within an hour, the *Greene* was standing by to render assistance to a brig ashore on Carysfort Reef.

Typical Salvage Events

When a wrecker sighted or received news of a ship aground, the captain would crowd on sail to be the first to arrive on the scene. On boarding the wreck, he would present his license to the master and offer his assistance. If the ship was in danger of breaking up or sinking, he would immediately take steps to transfer the passengers and crew to his wrecking vessel.

Typically, assuming there was no immediate danger to life, the master of the wrecked ship would refuse assistance, saying he intended to refloat his ship by himself. The wrecking captain would return to his vessel and stand by, knowing that the odds against the captain getting his ship off without help were extremely high.

When the next high tide had come and gone and the ship was still hard aground, her master would signal the wrecker that he was ready to accept help. Usually, by this time, several other wreckers would have arrived on the scene. The first-arrived captain was the wreck master and, as such, directed all the salvage operations and decided how many of the other wreckers, in the order in which they arrived, he needed to assist him. Either by a prior agreement or by one made on the spot, the wreck master and assisting wreckers would enter into a partnership, called a consortship, in which they agreed to share the salvage award. The usual basis was "ton for ton and man for man." This meant that half the total salvage award went to the vessels' owners, divided according to vessel tonnage, and half to the crews, divided according to the standard rule for distributing shares. A consortship agreement signed, witnessed, and certified by the clerk of the court and made in 1835 reads as follows:

> Know all men by these presents that I, Elum Eldridge, Master of the Licensed Wrecking Sloop *Mystic,* and George Eldridge, Master of the Licensed Wrecking Schooner *Whale*, have this day entered into a consortship for Six Months in the following conditions to wit. All monies

received for Salvage by ourselves or agents to be divided as follows. Schooner *Whale* & Sloop *Mystic* to draw equal as regards the vessels & Man for Man.

Key West, Mar. 20, 1835

In most cases, the first step in a salvage operation was to carry out and plant one or more anchors, both to prevent the ship from being driven further aground and to serve as a means to kedge (haul) the ship off after sufficient cargo had been offloaded. In the meantime, one or two wreckers would come alongside the wreck and begin breaking out and offloading cargo. If the water was too shallow alongside, the cargo would be transferred in the wreckers' boats. Speed was essential to get the ship off the reef before she bilged. Often, work went on around the clock for days.

At the next high tide, as many men as possible would man the wrecked ship's capstan or windlass and heave around. If enough cargo had been removed, the ship would slide off the reef. After the ship was afloat, depending on her condition, she would be sailed or towed to Key West.

Wreckers at work (*Harper's New Monthly Magazine*, Vol. 18, 1858/59, p. 577. Courtesy of Florida State Archives)

If the ship had bilged and was lost beyond recovery, the wrecking crews would remove the cargo and strip the rigging, sails, spars, anchors, deck gear, and other valuable items. Often divers would have to go down into the dark, water-filled cargo holds and, by feel alone, in water befouled by paints, dyes, and other toxic materials, wrestle out boxes, bales, and barrels.

Some salvage operations might last for several weeks and involve a dozen or more wreckers and more than a hundred men. Salvage of 3,432 cotton bales from the ship *Indian Hunter*, lost on French Reef in June 1856, required the combined efforts of 31 wrecking and fishing vessels and 259 men over a period of thirty days. Undoubtedly, the largest salvage operation was the recovery of cargo from the ship *Isaac Allerton*, sunk on Washerwoman Shoal off the Saddlebunch Keys in August 1856. Seventy-four craft, ranging from a 172-ton wrecking schooner to small row boats–or, as the judge of the admiralty court expressed it, "nearly or quite all the wrecking vessels and boats on the coast"–labored to extract cargo from the submerged hull for a period of two months.

Actual Salvage Operations

Every salvage situation was unique. Some posed great risk of injury or loss for wrecking personnel, their boats, and their vessels. Others forced the wreckers to invent new salvage methods or equipment on the spot. Some offered temptations that eventually resulted in forfeiture of salvage awards or even loss of wrecking licenses. The following true stories, taken from among 366 records of pre–Civil War wrecking court cases between 1831 and 1861, the heyday of the wrecking business, illustrate just a few of the many situations the Florida Keys wreckers faced and how they dealt with them.

Saving Lives

All wreckers were committed to the principle that their first duty on reaching the scene of a wrecked ship was to save the lives of the passengers and crew, even though they knew there would be no reward for doing so. Judge Marvin of the superior court at Key West wrote, "Risking life to save

Saving the lives of passengers and crew was the first duty of wreckers even though there was no reward for doing so. (*Harper's Weekly*, April 9, 1859. From the collections of The Mariners' Museum, Newport News, Virginia)

the property or lives of others is an ingredient in salvage service highly estimated. But the court has no authority to remunerate salvors for saving life merely." A reporter visiting Key West in 1854 wrote, "Much wrong has been done to the reputation of the Florida wreckers. In the exercise of their hard employment, they have never turned a deaf ear to the cries of humanity. They promptly leave their stations to carry ship-wrecked passengers into port, without remuneration; and often have they risked their lives to save strangers from a watery grave."

In April 1848, William Pent, captain of the eighty-ton, sixty-two-foot wrecking sloop *Ludlow*, sighted a ship ashore on Carysfort Reef and proceeded to render assistance. In a short while it became apparent that the ship had bilged and was leaking badly. Pent immediately ordered his crew to begin transferring the passengers, including a number of women, by boat to his sloop. Several hours later, the sloop *Texas* arrived and assisted in the transfer. When all twenty-seven passengers and their baggage were safely aboard, Pent took on what little salvaged cargo he had space left for and sailed to Key West. In their subsequent libel against the ship, all the wreckers involved relinquished any claim for a salvage award on the passengers' baggage they had saved. The judge allowed the *Ludlow* $50 for provisions consumed by the passengers during the five days they were aboard, but there was no reward for their rescue.

Capt. Henry Benners of the ninety-seven-ton wrecking schooner *James Webb* sighted the wreckage of a vessel on Sombrero Shoal in September 1837. On his way to her, he came upon a small raft with seven men, almost naked, delirious, and nearly dead. They said their schooner had been driven on the reef in a gale and they had been adrift on the raft without food or water for fifty-eight hours. They told Benners there were still some people, including women and children, on the wreck. The captain immediately launched his two boats to proceed ahead of the *James Webb* to the wreck. When they arrived, they found sixteen survivors clinging to the after part of the vessel, which was still out of water with the seas breaking over it. Some of the people were delirious, and all were in the last stages of exhaustion and despair. Among them were two slaves. The boat crews brought all the survivors safely back to the *James Webb*. In the subsequent court case, Benners claimed salvage against the two slaves on the grounds that they were part of the schooner's cargo. The captain of the schooner asserted they were passengers, not cargo. The judge sided with Benners and decreed that the slaves' owners must pay a salvage award of one-third of the value of the two slaves, which amounted to $500. Had it not been for the slaves, the *James Webb*'s crew would have received nothing for the rescue.

Saving the Vessel–the Ship Kestril

In many instances, it would have been to the wreckers' advantage to just save the cargo and let the ship go to pieces on the reef. This was especially true when the cargo was a valuable one, such as cotton, and the ship was not worth much in comparison. But to do so would have meant risking their salvage awards or even their licenses. If the admiralty court judge found that the wreckers had not used every available means to free the vessel or if he considered they had mismanaged the job through neglect or lack of skill, he would not hesitate to reduce their salvage awards. The wreckers were well aware of these policies and, as the following story illustrates, made every effort to refloat a wrecked ship even when it seemed beyond hope.

The British ship *Kestril*, with a full load of cotton bales in her hold and cedar logs on deck, was transiting the Straits of Florida on a voyage from New Orleans to Liverpool on August 9, 1848. At one o'clock in the morning, she struck the reef opposite Caesar's Creek. At daylight, James Bethel, captain of the seventy-four-ton, sixty-two-foot wrecking sloop *Empire*, sighted the ship and proceeded to her position. Bethel boarded the *Kestril*, presented his wrecking license to the master, and asked if he would accept assistance. The master declined, saying that he would try to get the ship off with out help from the wreckers. Bethel returned aboard his sloop and anchored

Launching a boat to take the captain, wrecking license in hand, to a wrecked ship (*The Century Illustrated Monthly Magazine,* Vol. XXIII, Nov. 1881 to Apr. 1882, p. 183. From the collections of The Mariners' Museum, Newport News, Virginia)

nearby to await further developments. A half-hour later, the thirty-one-ton, forty-six-foot wrecking sloop *Jane Eliza* arrived on the scene.

The wind was fresh and the sea rough. Both wrecking captains watched as the *Kestril's* seamen heaved the deck load of cedar logs overboard and her boat crews carried out two anchors. At three o'clock in the afternoon, the *Kestril's* crew hauled her afloat only to see her driven back on the reef when both anchor hawsers parted. Her boat crews then carried out two more anchors. In the process, one boat capsized, and the longboat's stern was smashed in against the side of the ship. The ship's crew heaved around on the capstan, but despite their best efforts, the ship would not come off a second time. Late in the afternoon, her master signaled the wreckers that he was ready to accept help.

The first wrecker alongside was the *Jane Eliza* with a crew of seven. To maneuver a sailing vessel alongside a wreck on the reef in strong winds and high seas required the highest degree of sailing skill and seamanship. The captain had to plan his approach carefully, taking into account all the elements: wind, current, depth of water, location of shoals, and orientation of the wreck. There was no engine to fall back on if he miscalculated, and only human muscle to handle sails and haul in lines and anchors. In certain situations, the captain might have only one chance to make a successful approach. Failure to evaluate one of the factors correctly could result in his own vessel being swept onto the reef.

If possible, the captain would plan to moor on the lee side (side away from wind) of the wreck in order to get some protection from the seas and to avoid being smashed against the wreck's hull. In a typical approach, the captain would head up into the wind near the wreck, drop an anchor, and drift back until he was close enough for his crew to throw over heaving lines. Sometimes it was necessary to take the lines over in a boat. Once the mooring lines were over, the wrecker's crew would haul their vessel alongside. When the wrecker was loaded, she would haul herself clear of the wreck by heaving in on her anchor hawser.

Jane Eliza's crew, along with most of the fourteen crewmen from the *Empire*, began breaking cotton bales out of the *Kestril's* hold and loading them aboard their sloop at nine o'clock at night. Several times, the work was interrupted as the surge of the seas caused mooring lines to part. At three in the morning, the wrecking sloops *Texas* and *Parallel*, each with a fourteen-man crew, arrived on the scene and sent men aboard to assist in the offloading.

Working through the night, the wreckers completed loading the *Jane Eliza* by seven o'clock in the morning. After she had hauled off and set sail for Key West, the *Empire* took her place alongside.

Later in the morning, a diver located one of the *Kestril*'s lost anchors and refastened the parted hawser to it. At high tide, the wreckers made their first attempt to haul the ship off the reef. The men at the capstan heaved around and succeeded in swinging the ship's bow into the seas. But almost immediately, the hawser parted, and the waves drove the ship broadside to the reef once more. The regrounding opened the ship's seams. By three o'clock in the afternoon, there was five feet of water in the hold, and the ship's master feared she would bilge. The wreckers and ship's crewmen manned the pumps in relays to keep them going continuously.

As the hours and then days passed, more wrecking vessels reached the scene. By the end of the second day, seven had arrived, and, by the end of the fifth day, a total of thirteen had come to share in the spoils. Bethel took all of them into the consortship under his authority as wreck master. Depending on the size of the wrecker and the number of men working, it took anywhere from six to twelve hours to load each wrecking vessel. As soon as one was loaded, hauled clear, and sailed for Key West, another took her place.

The weather was still rough. For seven hours on the fourth day, the wind and seas rose so high that none of the wreckers could get alongside. Mooring lines parted often. The wrecking vessels suffered damage, the *Empire* breaking off her topmast. Several boats capsized but were recovered, and no crewmen were lost. Throughout the entire operation, pumping never ceased, and the wreckers rarely slept.

On the morning of the third day, the wreck master ordered another attempt to haul the ship off. While the *Texas* was alongside loading, one of her boats carried out one of her anchors. There are several ways this could have been done. After the anchor was lowered to the boat, the boat crew might either sling it under the stern or lay it athwartships (at right angles to

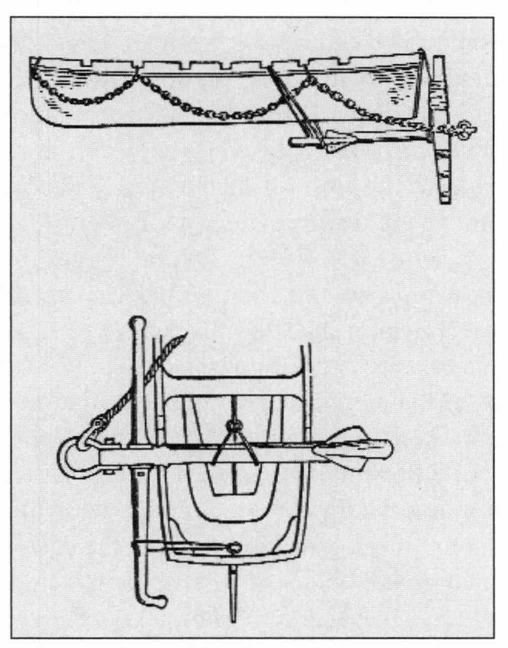

Two methods of carrying out an anchor by boat (*Manual for Naval Cadets*, J. M. Boyd, London, 1860. From the collections of The Mariners' Museum, Newport News, Virginia)

the keel), resting on the gunwales and two fore-and-aft beams. If the wind and current were setting in the direction the boat was to take the anchor, the men on the deck of the grounded vessel would pay out the anchor hawser as the boat crew rowed away. On reaching the designated spot for planting, the boat crew would either cut the lashings if the anchor was slung under the boat, or slide it off the stern if it was lying on the gunwales. If the boat had to be rowed against the wind and current, the boat crew would coil the hawser in the boat, row to the designated spot, plant the anchor with the hawser attached, then pay out the hawser as they rowed back to the vessel on the reef. After *Texas*'s anchor was planted, as many men as possible manned the capstan and heaved around, but the *Kestril* still would not move.

By the afternoon of the sixth day, the wreckers had offloaded fourteen hundred bales of cotton, and the wreck master decided to make another attempt to heave the ship off using one of the *Kestril*'s bower (largest) anchors and anchor chain. The bower anchor was much too heavy (about three thousand pounds) to be carried out by boat. The captain of one of the smaller wreckers, the thirty-six-ton, forty-six-foot *Harriet B. Hawkins*, maneuvered his sloop to a position such that his stern was under the starboard bow of the *Kestril.* The ship's crew lowered the bower anchor, and seamen on the *Hawkins* slung it to the stern of their vessel. The *Hawkins'* crew then hauled their sloop out to the designated spot for planting, using the anchor dropped during her approach. Next, several boats working together attached floats to the *Kestril's* anchor chain to buoy it up and towed it out to the *Hawkins. Hawkins'* crewmen shackled the chain to the bower anchor and cut the anchor loose.

As the tide rose, as many men as possible heaved around on the *Kestril's* capstan. At five o'clock in the evening, the *Kestril* slid off the reef. By anchoring a sloop to seaward and running lines to her from the ship, the wreckers hauled the *Kestril* into deep water and anchored her for the night.

Shepherded by one of the wrecking vessels, the *Kestril* set sail for Key West. Because of unfavorable winds, it was six days before she arrived. In the subsequent court case, the *Kestril's* master acknowledged that the wreckers had saved his ship, but complained that they had not exercised sufficient care in breaking out the cotton bales. (In order to load the maximum number of bales, it was common practice to compress them into the hold with jack screws). Judge Marvin awarded the wreckers one-third of the value of the ship and cargo, which amounted to $13,697. Half of that amount went to the wrecking vessel owners. The other half, divided among 140 crewmen, gave them shares of about $38. As it turned out, the wreckers' efforts to save the ship were wasted. Surveyors concluded that the ship was unworthy of repair.

Saving the Cargo–the Ship Telamon

Despite their best efforts, the wreckers did not always save the wrecked ship. Early in the morning of January 12, 1852, the ship *Telamon*, on a voyage from New York to New Orleans with a cargo of assorted goods, ran aground on Delta Shoals off Key Vaca. At ten o'clock in the morning, William Lowe, captain of the wrecking schooner *Lizzy Wall*, sighted the ship and proceeded to her position.

Wreckers removing cargo from hold of wrecked ship (redrawn by Wayne Giordano from an illustration in *The Illustrated London News,* Vol. 17, 1850. From the collections of The Mariners' Museum, Newport News, Virginia)

At first, the *Telamon's* master refused assistance and attempted to force his ship off the reef with the sails. When he realized it was useless, he signaled the *Lizzy Wall* that he was ready to accept assistance. In the meantime, two other wrecking vessels had arrived, and Lowe directed the smaller of the two to go alongside and begin offloading. As the day wore on, more wrecking vessels and several fishing craft arrived on the scene.

The rough weather precluded the use of boats, so one of the smaller wrecking vessels carried out two large anchors. At one o'clock in the afternoon of the second day, the wreckers succeeded in hauling the ship off the reef and heaved her to within sixty feet of one of the anchors. Another wrecker anchored further off the reef and ran a long hawser back to the ship with which to haul her out to deep water. Just as this was completed, the wind suddenly rose to gale force and drove the ship back on the reef, dragging the wrecking vessel with her. The strong winds and heavy seas forced the wreckers to run for shelter among the Keys, leaving thirteen of their crewmen stranded on the *Telamon.* These men, together with the ship's crew, continued pumping all night.

The next day, the wind moderated slightly, and the wreckers returned. The sixty-ton, sixty-four-foot schooner *William Chestnut* attempted to go alongside, but a powerful current swept her rapidly toward the ship. Only the anchor she dropped during the approach saved her from being smashed against the *Telamon*'s hull.

The waves rolled the *Telamon* from side to side and plunged her up and down, causing her to pound on the bottom. The motion was so violent that the men on deck had to hold on, and the men working in the rigging had to descend. Down in the hold, boxes and barrels slid and rolled about, forcing the men to abandon any further efforts to get cargo up on deck.

As the pounding on the bottom continued, water flooded into the hold faster than the pumps could keep up with it. Convinced the ship had bilged, the men quit the pumps. On the fourth day, one wrecking vessel managed to get alongside and offload some cargo, but it was still too rough to send men into the lower hold.

The wind and seas finally moderated on the fifth day. The ship now lay over on her starboard side. The wrecking crews used hooks at the end of long poles to drag out some of the cargo floating in the hold. They also cut holes in the deck to gain access to areas of the hold away from the hatches.

By the eighth day, all the cargo that could be reached from topside had been removed. Twelve divers from the wreckers began work in what was one of the coldest Januarys on record. The water was so cold that the divers could make only two or three dives before they were forced to stop and allow their bodies to warm up for several hours. The water they had to work in was black and fouled with drugs, dye stuffs, oil, lamp black, paint, and other noxious substances. For three weeks, the divers continued their labors. In the process, all of them became ill with chills and fever.

Despite the hopeless situation of his ship, the *Telamon*'s master was not yet willing to abandon her. At his urging and despite their better judgment, the wreckers sent to Key West for two windmill pumps at a cost to them of $900. With both windmills in operation and as many men as possible working the ship's pumps, there was no decrease in the water level after twenty-four hours of effort.

The wreck master next devised a plan to roll the ship over onto her port side, cover the holes in the starboard bilge with canvas, and then pump the ship out. From Key West, he obtained two derricks and three ship's purchases (heavy-duty block and tackle rigs). Wrecking crewmen set one end of each derrick on the bottom alongside the ship and rigged purchases from the top ends so as to exert a lifting force on the starboard side of the ship. One of the wrecking vessels planted the ship's thirty-five-hundred-pound anchor about five hundred feet off the port side and ran a line from the anchor chain over the mainmast and down to the third purchase. The wreckers ran the hauling parts of the purchases to the ship's capstans and heaved around. After several hours of heaving without success, it was evident that they could not roll the ship over.

The *Telamon*'s master was still not ready to give up, hoping that two steam pumps ordered from New York would arrive in time to save his ship. But on March 3, almost four weeks after the ship went aground, a strong wind blowing out of the southwest began raising heavy swells. The ship pounded so heavily that the decks, knees, and other timbers began to break. Realizing all was lost, the master gave permission to the wreckers to strip the ship of her rigging, sails, anchors, furnishings, and other items of value.

Despite extraordinary efforts, seven regular wrecking vessels and ten fishing craft with a total of 123 men had failed to save the *Telamon* but had salvaged most of her cargo and materials under difficult conditions. Judge Marvin awarded the salvors approximately one-third of the value of the cargo and materials saved, appraised at $37,249.

Riding Out a Gale—the Ship Lucy

On another stormy day in January just one year later, a consortship of ten wrecking vessels and four fishing and turtling craft succeeded in hauling the ship *Lucy* off Looe Key reef. They had worked unceasingly for five days, offloading 1,534 bales of cotton, carrying out anchors, and heaving around at the windlass. With the aid of the sails, they had gotten the ship about two hundred yards from the reef when the wind suddenly shifted, caught the sails aback, and drove the ship astern toward the coral heads. The crew immediately let go the last anchor, and the *Lucy* brought up just a short distance from the edge of the reef.

By nightfall, the wind was blowing at gale force, and all the wrecking vessels ran for sheltered anchorages. (*Harper's New Monthly Magazine*, Vol. XV, June 1857, p. 754. From the collections of The Mariners' Museum, Newport News, Virginia)

By nightfall, the wind was blowing at gale force, and all the wrecking vessels ran for sheltered anchorages. Sixteen crewmen from the wreckers were left on board the *Lucy* in addition to her regular crew of twenty-two. The men took turns at the pumps to keep up with the leaks. The wind force continued to increase as the night wore on. When the stern began striking the bottom at one o'clock in the morning, the crew heaved in a few fathoms of chain to haul clear, but no more for fear of breaking the anchor's hold.

At daylight, a full gale was blowing, interspersed with violent squalls. The ship's stern was just fifty yards from the breakers crashing over the reef, and there were more breakers on either side. John Smith, the wreck master and captain of the wrecking schooner *Dart*, advised *Lucy's* master to cut away the masts to save the ship and their lives. After the masts went overboard, the ship rode more easily, but she had dragged closer to the reef and began striking aft again. Once more, the men heaved in chain until she stopped striking and then held their breath until they were certain the anchor was holding.

At eight o'clock in the morning, with the wind still increasing, the barometer falling, and tremendous breakers all around the ship, Captain

Smith fully expected the chain to part at any moment. In the afternoon, the breakers were half-mast high, and the ship was rolling so heavily that the men could hardly keep their feet. In the cabin, dishes, cups, jugs, books–everything that was not securely fastened down–crashed down, broke, and rolled or slid about the deck.

At three o'clock that afternoon, the anchor dragged again, then caught. The wreck master ordered the men at the anchor windlass to heave in a few more fathoms of chain to prevent her striking aft. As the afternoon wore on, the wind and seas began to moderate, giving hope to everyone that the end of their ordeal might be in sight.

But at two o'clock in the morning on the second day of the storm, the wind shifted to a more southerly direction, swinging the stern of the *Lucy* closer to the reef. The stern began to strike the bottom again, so Smith

The wreck master advised the *Lucy*'s master to cut away the masts to save the ship and their lives. (*Harper's Weekly*, Vol. 3, May 12, 1860, p. 301. From the collections of The Mariner's Museum, Newport News, Virginia)

ordered the crew to heave in eight more fathoms of chain. This left only thirty fathoms of chain to the anchor. The stern continued to strike, but not so heavily.

At daylight, the pounding on the bottom had become heavier, but the wreck master was afraid to heave in any more chain. Fortunately, an hour later the wind shifted more to the west and swung the stern clear of the bottom, but then began to blow as hard as it had the previous day. The ship was now in the trough of the seas and rolling dreadfully. At noon, the wind began to moderate and the barometer started to rise, but at three o'clock, the winds and sea picked up again and periodically the ship would strike the bottom.

The gale finally subsided at four o'clock in the morning of the third day. The wind moderated rapidly and shifted to the north, swinging the ship's stern clear of the bottom. At daylight, the *Dart* and three other wrecking vessels came out to the reef and, after the *Lucy's* crew had weighed anchor, took her in tow to Key West. Inspection of the anchor showed that it was severely bent, indicating that it had caught under a rock. This was the only reason the ship was able to ride out the gale with such a short scope of chain.

Judge Marvin awarded the salvors twenty percent of the value of the ship and her cargo, or $30,700. Individual shares amounted to about $110. Noting that it was one of the largest salvage awards made in the history of the court, he commented that it was justified by the "considerable peril" to which the salvors were exposed during the gale.

Damage and Losses

In the course of salvage operations, particularly in rough weather, the wrecking vessels suffered much damage. Sails split, masts cracked, topmasts were carried away, boat davits and rails were torn away, lines parted, anchors were lost, windlasses broke, rudders unshipped, and holes were stove in sides. Boats capsized, were stove in, were swamped with the weight of anchors, or were smashed to pieces against coral heads. Yet despite all the damage to vessels, boats, and equipment, there is not a single report of loss of life in all the pre–Civil War wrecking court records.

Further evidence of the seamanship skills of the wreckers is demonstrated by the fact that, in the pre–Civil War wrecking court records, there are only three instances of the loss of a wrecking vessel during salvage operations. One of these occurred in 1836 when the forty-five-ton sloop *Thistle*, having completed offloading cargo, hauled away from the side of the wreck and struck an anchor laying on the bottom. The stock of the anchor drove a hole through her bottom and she sank and was not recovered. The wrecking schooner *Pizarro* was assisting the brig *Sea Drift*, aground inside the reef at Old Rhodes Creek in September 1835, when hurricane winds drove her ashore. She was a total loss.

The third major casualty during salvage operations was the loss of the Key West–built, 132-ton, 90-foot pilot schooner *Florida* by fire in 1857. The *Florida's* crew had offloaded 250 bales of cotton from a ship ashore on Ajax Reef when she began to pound on the bottom. The wreck master decided it would be best to remove some of the cotton from the *Florida* before trying to haul her away from the side of the wreck. He directed the *Texas* to come alongside the *Florida* for this purpose. By this time it was dark, and the wrecking crewmen placed lanterns about the deck to illuminate their work. One of the men, crossing the *Florida's* deck to the *Texas*, kicked a lantern over, breaking it and setting the cotton on fire. Because the *Florida* was sandwiched between the wrecked ship and the *Texas*, there was no quick way to heave the burning cotton overboard. In order to save the other vessels, crewmen cut the *Florida* loose and abandoned her. She drifted away and burned until she sank.

The hurricane of September 1835 cast at least a dozen ships up on the reef, several of them total losses, and there were a number of casualties among the wrecking vessels as well. The loss of the schooner *Pizarro* during the storm has already been mentioned. The schooner *Brilliant* lost her anchor and sank at Key Vaca, while the schooners *Caroline* and *Florida* both lost masts. Another wrecking schooner was driven ashore and, when the wind abated, was left high and dry. Undaunted by this predicament, the captain and his crew of eleven men dug a canal two hundred yards long, got their vessel afloat, and proceeded to salvage one of the wrecks. Another wrecking vessel lost both masts, her anchors, cables, boats, and spare rigging. But, as a Key West newspaper reporter put it, "The conviction that he had nothing more to lose seems to have roused her stout-hearted master to greater exertion; and with the aid of two small jury-masts, and an old gun for an anchor, he succeeded in reaching a wreck and relieved her of a large and valuable cargo."

The hurricane of 1846, the worst ever to strike Key West, drove the schooner *Eliza Catherine* ashore at Key Vaca and sank the schooners *Lafayette* and *Louisa* at Key West. The *Lafayette* was lost with all hands. As previously related, the *Louisa* was raised and sailed again. Considering there were close to thirty full-time wrecking vessels at this time, it is remarkable that no more were lost.

In the course of salvage operations, particularly in rough weather, wrecking vessels suffered much damage. (*Chronicles of the Sea*, No. 58, Dec. 15, 1838, p. 457. From the collections of The Mariners' Museum, Newport News, Virginia)

Chapter 7

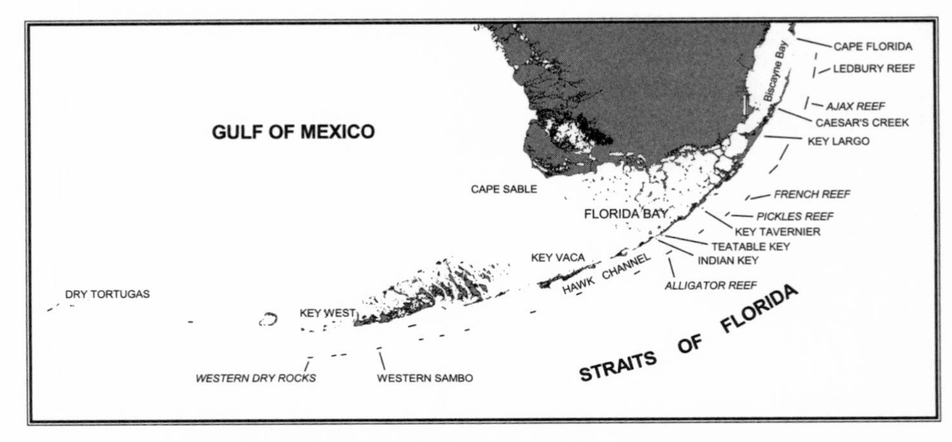

The Florida Keys and the Florida Reef (drawing by Erich Mueller)

UNUSUAL SALVAGE OPERATIONS

Hostile Natives

Gales were not the only hazard the wreckers faced. During the early years of the Second Seminole War (1836–1842), the Seminole Indians maintained undisputed control of south Florida, and their war parties made several raids into the upper Keys. Despite the danger of Indian attack, the wreckers continued to patrol the reef and the southern mainland coast.

Evidence that wrecking vessels in the upper Keys and along the south Florida coast were not immune from attack came in October 1836. A small turtling-wrecking schooner, the *Mary,* was anchored at Key Tavernier when a crewman sighted a party of thirty Indians in dugout canoes approaching rapidly. *Mary's* five-man crew hastily abandoned their vessel in two small boats and began rowing for their lives. The Indians opened fire, wounding two of the seamen. But on reaching the schooner, the warriors turned their energies to plundering and, when they had finished, set the vessel on fire. The crew reached safety, but their vessel was lost.

There were no further over-water attacks against vessels in the Keys, but in February 1839, a wrecker salvaging cotton from a brig ashore fifty miles north of Cape Florida discovered evidence of a planned ambush from the beach. The wrecking vessel had been forced to run for shelter because of a gale, leaving one of its crewmen and the crew of the brig behind on board the brig. When the wreckers returned, they found that the Seminoles had taken some of the cotton left on the beach and had cleared lines of fire through the brush in the direction of the wrecked brig. They had also planted stakes with crotches on which to rest their rifles. Apparently the return of the wrecking vessel convinced them to abandon the attack.

At the time of the Seminole raid on Indian Key in 1840, a wrecking sloop was moored at the end of one of the wharves. The sounds of gunshots and war whoops in the early morning hours awakened the crew to the attack. The captain and mate lowered a hatch cover over the side and paddled to the safety of a schooner anchored by Tea Table Key about a mile away. The rest of the crew ran ashore to find hiding places. All but one crawled under the shoreward end of the wharf and piled up some rocks to conceal themselves. The remaining seaman followed a resident and a young boy who were headed for a warehouse used for storing salvaged cargoes. The two men and the boy hid in a cistern under the warehouse. The next afternoon, the Indians set fire to the warehouse and nearly all the other buildings on the island. The two men climbed out of the cistern and escaped through the flames, but the boy died in the cistern, presumably of suffocation.

Unusual Salvage Methods

Wrecking captains often had to employ unusual or unique methods in order to save a ship or its cargo. If the weather was too rough or the water too shallow to get alongside the wreck, they used their boats to transfer the cargo. This was a slow and often hazardous method. In heavy weather, it might be impossible to row the boats against the winds and seas. The captain would then anchor his wrecker up wind and sea, run lines between his vessel and the wreck, and haul the boats back and forth.

Often when a ship was driven onto the reef, the rudder would break away from its fittings. After cargo had been removed and the ship kedged into deeper water, divers would go down to reattach the rudder. This oper-

In heavy weather, it might be impossible to row the boats against the winds and sea (*Scribner's Magazine*, Vol. III, January–June 1888, p. 526. From the collections of The Mariners' Museum, Newport News, Virginia)

ation required expert rigging of supporting lines and blocks and tackles to assist the divers to maneuver the large, heavy rudders into position. If the rudder was lost or the fittings damaged beyond repair, the ship would have to be towed back to Key West. One wrecking vessel would take position ahead to tow. A second would take position astern and, by means of a line from the stern of the ship to its bow, maneuver so as to steer the ship.

Sometimes when the wreckers were attempting to kedge a ship off the reef, the anchor would break out of the bottom and come home, that is, be dragged back to the ship. To give the anchor greater holding power, a boat crew would plant a second anchor some distance beyond it. A diver would take the hawser from the second anchor, swim down, haul it taut, and fasten it to the exposed arm and fluke of the first anchor. This operation was known as "backing" an anchor.

To get better holding power for kedging a vessel off the reef, two wreckers would anchor in tandem. In preparation for hauling the schooner *St. Marys* off the Western Sand Bore (Western Sambo today) in 1847,

Captain Geiger anchored his wrecking schooner *Louisa* with two anchors 150 yards astern of the *St. Marys.* Captain Alderslade in the wrecking schooner *Lafayette* then anchored four hundred yards beyond the *Louisa.* Boat crews ran a hawser from the *Lafayette* to the *Louisa* and another hawser from the *Louisa* to the windlass of the grounded schooner. In a very short time, the crew of the *St. Marys* heaved themselves afloat.

When a ship was bilged and lost beyond any hope of recovery, the wreckers would use more drastic measures to remove the cargo. A good example of this was the salvage of the cargo of the bark *Yucatan,* ashore and bilged on French Reef in 1847. The cargo consisted of nearly twelve hundred bales of cotton plus meat, flour, and corn. Stormy weather hampered and sometimes forced suspension of operations by the ten wrecking vessels involved. When it was possible, the wreckers boated the cargo off; at other times they heaved bales of cotton overboard and recovered them in the calmer waters inside the reef. After four days, the wind moderated sufficiently to allow one of the wrecking vessels to get alongside. But the hold was full of water and the cargo so jammed in that it was almost impossible to extract. The wreckers cut away part of the deck and beams to make access easier.

When a ship was bilged and beyond hope of recovery, wreckers would use more drastic measures to remove the cargo (*The Illustrated London News*, Vol. 16, April 13, 1850, p. 244. From the collections of The Mariners' Museum, Newport News, Virginia)

On the sixth day, the corn began to ferment and the fumes blinded the men trying to work in the hold. With only about a third of the cargo removed and almost thirty men blinded by the fermenting corn, the wreck master obtained the master's permission to set the ship on fire. The fire burned the ship's upper works down to the waterline, allowing freer access for men and air to enter the hold. The divers went back to work, but not before they demanded and received promises of extra compensation. Another twelve days passed before they finished removing all but a very small portion of the cargo.

The extraordinary measures wreckers sometimes resorted to in order to free a vessel from the grip of the reef are well illustrated by the salvage of the steamer *Anglo Saxon,* which went ashore on Ledbury Reef fifteen miles south of Cape Florida in December 1848. William H. Bethel, captain of the wrecking sloop *Texas,* was first on the scene and formed a consortship with the wrecking sloops *Parallel* and *Randall H. Green,* which arrived soon thereafter.

After taking soundings around the steamer, Bethel determined the best way to free her would be to force the ship's head around to starboard and haul her off astern to the inside of the reef. Six times during the first two days, wrecking crewmen carried out, planted, and heaved around on anchors to no avail. Other men shifted some of the coal in the steamer from aft to forward and heaved more of it over the side. To help the anchors force the steamer around, the wreckers rigged a spare spar on the starboard side of the bow as a derrick to exert a lifting force on the forward end of the steamer. They set one end in the bottom, attached a heavy-duty block and tackle to the upper end, and ran the hauling part to the windlass. By heaving on the derrick line while simultaneously heaving in on the anchor hawsers, they managed to force the ship's head around about eleven degrees.

On the third day, boat crews replanted one of the anchors that had dragged and planted another to back the two anchors astern. At low tide, a group of men went overboard and dug away a ridge of rocks that had piled up on the starboard side of the steamer. Bethel sent the *Randall H. Green* to Cape Florida to get the mast from a wrecked smack he knew was there. When she returned, the wreckers rigged the mast as a second derrick at the bow. Once again the men heaved on the derrick and anchor lines but were able to move the steamer only a few feet.

During the night, the smaller derrick broke while the men were heaving on it, but Bethel had no intention of quitting. In the morning, he repositioned the large derrick over the bow and ran a chain from the three anchors astern through the steamer's machinery space to the forward windlass. At nine o'clock, with the men heaving a heavy strain on the derrick's block and tackle line and the stern anchor chain, they hauled the steamer afloat. The three wrecking sloops then hooked themselves together and, with the steamer in tow, brought her safely to Key West. For their unusual and determined efforts, Judge Marvin awarded the salvagers forty percent of the value of the steamer and its cargo–$12,000.

Strange Cargoes

The most common cargoes wreckers had to deal with were cotton, sugar, molasses, tobacco, cigars, lumber, coffee, and miscellaneous merchandise such as clothing, furniture, and hardware. But, occasionally, some real surprises greeted the wreckers when they opened the cargo hatches.

In 1827, the ship *Spermo* ran ashore on Alligator Reef and was a total loss. Amidst the cargo saved was a strange-looking bundle that gave off a foul odor. Authorities in Key West identified it as an Egyptian mummy. Stripping off the many layers of linen cloth, they found a skeleton with a dislocated neck. The smell was so offensive that the collector of customs ordered the mummy burned, and there was no salvage award for it.

More bones, this time in boxes, turned up in cargo salvaged from the wreck of the ship *Newark,* lost on Pickles Reef in 1845. But they were not human bones, and they did not resemble the bones of any known animal. The mystery was finally solved by a communication from the frantic owner of the bones, Dr. Albert C. Koch, a famed paleontologist. He explained that they were the fossilized remains of a prehistoric sea monster that he had discovered during a dig in Alabama and had named "hydrarchos." When alive, the hydrarchos was over 140 feet long and 30 feet in circumference. Dr. Koch was concerned that the bones would be discarded or that he would have to pay a large salvage award he could not afford. His fears were eased when he learned that the bones were intact; that Judge Marvin had ruled

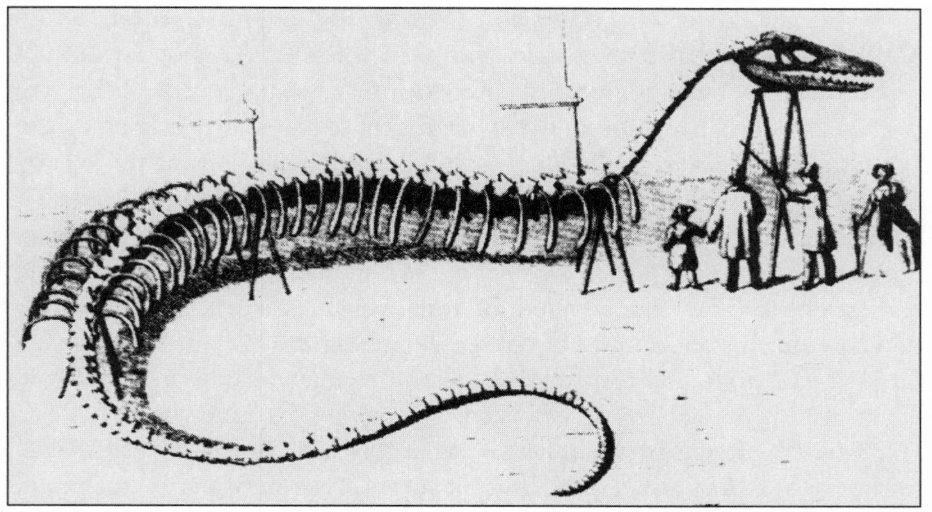

Bones of the prehistoric sea monster hydrarchos were salvaged from a shipwreck on the Florida Reef in 1845. (*Journey Through a Part of the United States of North America in the Years 1844 to 1846* by Dr. Albert C. Koch. Courtesy of Monroe County Public Library)

that the bones had no monetary value but were of great value to the scientific world; and that the wreckers had withdrawn any claim for salvage on them.

After he received the bones, Dr. Koch wrote in his diary, "Conscientiously, those noble-minded men kept their promise, so that some time later I had the great pleasure of exhibiting Hydrarchos. . . ." During the exhibition, the doctor was visited by the captain of the *Newark,* who told him that during the transfer of the boxes from the ship to one of the wrecking vessels, one of the boxes fell overboard. The wind was blowing hard and the waves were steep and breaking. Nevertheless, as Dr. Koch described it in his diary, "a wrecker, without prolonged reflection, tied one end of a long rope to the boat and, with the other end in his hand, jumped into the waves, under which he immediately disappeared. But shortly he again appeared at the ocean's surface and was grasped by one of his comrades, while others tried to pull up the box which was attached to the rope from the ocean floor. Certainly, this case, in which wreckers salvaged an item which would have been lost forever without their help, not to acquire money, but solely to do science a service, deserves to be generally known."

The captains of *Dart, Champion, Lafayette,* and *Empire* faced one of the biggest challenges of their wrecking careers when they pondered how to recover a locomotive engine and railroad iron from the wreck of the brig *Cimbrus.* The brig had sunk in twenty-eight feet of water after bilging on the Western Dry Rocks in 1853. They solved the problem of raising the iron by fabricating long poles with tongs at one end to grasp and hoist the iron bars. To recover the engine, they fitted an old brig with sheers (two or three spars raised at an angle and lashed together at the top) and attached a heavy block and tackle rig. They maneuvered the brig over the locomotive, sent divers down to attach a sling, and hoisted the engine off the bottom. They towed the brig back to a wharf in Key West with the engine slung underneath it. Then, with "great labor," they hoisted the engine up on the wharf.

Faced with the problem of saving eighty-nine horses on the Army transport *Sparkling Sea* in 1863, the wreckers were only partly successful because of rough weather. Four days after the transport went aground on Ajax Reef, the wreckers got the troops safely off, but the horses were still on board, and the ship was beginning to break up. Another four days passed before the schooner *Magnolia* was able to get alongside and hoist off thirteen horses. The next day, the wreckers got eighteen horses up on the deck of the transport but were unable to bring a schooner alongside because of the rough weather. Finally, on the thirteenth day after the wreck, they managed to take off one more horse, the last one still alive.

Slavers Turn the Tables on Salvors

The first faint light of dawn on December 20, 1827, revealed the silhouettes of three sailing vessels anchored at the mouth of Caesar's Creek in the upper Keys. Two of them, the schooner *Thorn* and the sloop *Surprize,* were wreckers; the third, the *Florida,* was a fishing smack. *Thorn* and *Surprize* were members of a consortship that included two other wrecking vessels, the sloop *Capital,* anchored thirty miles to the southwest at Key Tavernier, and the schooner *General Geddes,* then making her way up the reef to join her consorts. These five vessels were about to become involved in the strangest salvage operation in Florida Keys wrecking history.

As the light grew stronger, the watch on deck of the *Thorn* called the

In a matter of minutes, *Thorn*'s crewmen were heaving in the anchor and hoisting sails as the schooner gathered way in the stiff morning breeze (*The Century Magazine*, Vol. XXVII, April 1884, No. 6, p. 889. From the collections of the Mariners' Museum, Newport News, Virginia)

captain, Charles Grover, to come topside and take a look at two dim shapes he could see on the horizon. Through his spyglass, Grover made out that one was a schooner, not moving but with her main and foresail up. Nearby was a larger vessel with no masts visible, lying low in the water. In a matter of minutes, *Thorn*'s crewmen were heaving in the anchor and hoisting sails as the schooner gathered way in the stiff morning breeze. In a very short while, *Surprize* and *Florida* also got under way and followed *Thorn* out to the two wrecks on the reef, about five miles distant.

As the *Thorn* drew near the wrecked vessels, Grover could see that the bigger one was a brig heeled over to one side, her masts gone. A large number of men clung to ropes strung along the deck as the seas broke over them. Grover anchored in the lee of the wreck and ordered one of his boats lowered. Telling his mate to take charge of saving the brig's crew, Grover and two of his crewmen rowed towards the other wrecked vessel, a schooner, about two and a half miles away.

After Grover had left, a boat from the brig came alongside the *Thorn,* bringing a man who identified himself as Jose Gomez, captain of the Spanish brig *Guerrero.* He said he had a crew of ninety men and a cargo of some five hundred Africans bound for the slave market in Cuba. Gomez told the mate that the wrecked schooner was a British Navy man-of-war on anti-slavery patrol. The British had sighted his brig on the edge of the Bahama Bank the previous day and had chased her across the Straits. As night fell, the schooner overtook the slave brig and the two vessels engaged each other in a gun battle for about a half hour. The wind was strong and there were heavy swells. Endeavoring to escape, Gomez put the brig before the wind with all sails set. Forty-five minutes later, the brig struck the reef with such force that both masts went overboard, and the cargo hold began to flood rapidly. As the water rushed in, screams of horror arose from below decks. Before the crew could release them from their irons, forty-one of the Africans drowned.

Gomez said that no one from the British schooner had boarded him as yet, and, therefore, as the *Thorn* was the first vessel to come to his aid, he considered himself a prize to her. He begged the mate to save his crew and the Africans and to protect them from the British. He also asked the mate to hoist an American flag on the brig to show that it was a prize to an American vessel.

By 1827, the United States, Britain, and Spain had outlawed the slave trade, and both American and British naval vessels patrolled the coast of Africa and approaches to the Caribbean and Gulf of Mexico to apprehend slave vessels. It was apparent that Gomez preferred to take his chances with the American wreckers than with the sailors and marines of a British man-of-war and was probably already plotting an escape from his predicament.

In the meantime, Grover had reached the wrecked schooner and learned that it was His British Majesty's Schooner *Nimble,* Lt. Edward Holland commanding, with a crew of thirty-six seamen and marines. Holland told Grover that after a half-hour engagement with the slave brig, her captain had indicated surrender by ceasing fire, firing a gun to leeward, and showing a light. As a result, Holland considered the brig his prize.

Grover asked Holland if he wished any assistance to help get the schooner off the reef. Holland replied that he would appreciate aid as soon as possible. The *Nimble*'s crew were preparing to heave their largest gun, an eighteen-pound pivot gun, over the side. Grover said he would have his consort, the *Surprize,* now approaching the scene, come alongside, take the gun aboard, and assist in getting the *Nimble* afloat. Holland ordered two of the British seamen to go with Grover to expedite rowing to the *Surprize.* On reaching her, Grover asked her captain, Samuel Sanderson, to go to the *Nimble*'s aid, then rowed back to the *Thorn.*

Once Sanderson had moored the *Surprize* alongside the *Nimble,* his crew went to work to take aboard the pivot gun. They also discovered that *Nimble*'s rudder and false keel had been torn off and realized that further lightening would be necessary to get her afloat. Together with the *Nimble*'s crew, they heaved shot and kentledge (ballast) over the side, then secured a towing hawser between *Nimble*'s bow and *Surprize*'s stern. *Surprize*'s crew hoisted sail, and the sloop got under way to try to tow the schooner afloat. As the breeze freshened and the tide rose, the *Nimble* slipped off the reef. Sanderson towed her into deeper water inside the reef, then, calling to Holland to drop anchor, cast off the tow line.

While the *Surprize* was engaged in getting the *Nimble* afloat, *Thorn*'s crewmen were busy transferring Spanish crewmen and Africans from the *Guerrero* to the *Thorn* in their boats. When the fishing smack *Florida* arrived on the scene, Grover, now back aboard the *Thorn,* asked her captain, Austin Packer, to help in saving people from the brig. Even with the *Florida*'s help, there was no possibility that two wrecking vessels could take aboard some 550 Africans and Spanish crewmen. Grover, seeing that the *Nimble* was afloat and safely anchored, sent his mate in a boat to find out why the *Surprize* was not coming to help get people off the brig. On reaching the *Surprize,* the mate learned that her main boom had broken during a sudden shift in the wind and that the crew was in the process of repairing it.

At eleven o'clock in the morning, Holland, accompanied by one of his officers and six of his men, rowed to the *Surprize* and asked Sanderson to take him, his men, and his boat to the wreck of the slaver. As soon as the boom was repaired, Sanderson got under way with *Nimble*'s boat in tow and then anchored close by the *Guerrero.* Holland boarded the *Thorn* and found that her crew had taken a number of muskets from the brig. Concerned that the slaver's crewmen might get hold of them, he ordered his men to disable them by firing them and dipping them in water.

With their holds and decks crowded with Spanish crewmen and Africans, there was no possibility that either of the wrecking vessels or the fishing smack could salvage any of the rigging, sails, and other valuable materials that might be aboard the *Guerrero.* Accordingly, at one o'clock in the afternoon, Grover sent a boat to find the schooner *General Geddes* and tell her to crowd on sail to arrive as soon as possible.

When the *Florida* had taken aboard 146 Africans and about 25 Spaniards, she got under way, presumably headed for Key West. What happened thereafter is not known. Fishing smacks had small crews, typically five or six men. It would have been easy for twenty-five desperate Spaniards to overpower the crew, and this is the generally accepted theory as to what happened. It is also possible that the Spanish officers offered Packer a monetary reward if he would carry the Africans to Cuba. In any event, once out of sight of the vessels at the wreck, the *Florida* changed course for Cuba, either unwillingly or willingly.

By four o'clock in the afternoon, Grover had taken 252 Africans and 54 Spaniards aboard the *Thorn,* all the schooner could hold. To forestall any attempt by the Spaniards to seize the *Thorn* by force, Holland asked Grover to anchor under the *Nimble's* guns during the night. With great difficulty because of the crowded deck, Grover got his schooner under way and anchored close aboard the *Nimble.* Holland and three of his men rode back to their ship aboard the *Thorn,* leaving a British officer and three men in the *Nimble's* boat at the brig.

All the remaining people from the slaver, 121 Africans and 12 Spanish crewmen, had been put aboard the *Surprize.* Although Sanderson does not mention the incident in his deposition, there must have been an attempt by the Spaniards to take over the sloop sometime in the afternoon. In the fight, one of *Surprize's* crewmen suffered a bullet wound and another a stab wound. As a result, there were not enough able seamen to get the *Surprize* under way to follow the *Thorn* to the protection of the *Nimble's* guns.

By the time the *Thorn* anchored near the *Nimble,* her consort, the schooner *General Geddes,* had reached the scene. Grover directed her captain, John Morrison, to proceed to the wreck of the brig, to anchor close to the *Surprize* to give her protection from a possible uprising by the Spaniards, and to begin salvaging materials from the wreck. Morrison, realizing he would need more help for the salvage work, sent a boat to Key Tavernier to ask the fourth consort, the sloop *Capital,* to come to the scene.

Anticipating a change in wind direction that might cause the *Nimble* to swing and foul his anchor cable, Grover decided to shift the *Thorn*'s anchorage a little way astern of the man-of-war. It was a fateful decision. At eight o'clock, the night was dark, and Grover and his mate were in the cabin eating supper. The mate heard the schooner's boat, which should have been trailing astern, bumping against the hull. He sprang up the companionway, ran forward, and found that the anchor cable had been cut and the *Thorn* was adrift. He immediately let go the other anchor and, as he did so, heard the sound of sails being raised. Just as he was taking a turn around the bitts with the anchor cable, he saw several Spaniards rushing towards him. He and another seaman ran towards the companionway, only to find it surrounded by more Spaniards. Seeing no chance to avoid being captured, both men jumped overboard and swam to the *Nimble.* The Spaniards slipped the *Thorn*'s anchor cable, finished raising the sails, and the schooner began to glide away.

The *Nimble*'s boat picked up the two men from the water, and after the mate told the British officer what had happened, began rowing after the *Thorn* and firing at her. Sailors on the *Nimble* also fired a musket volley, but it was to no avail; the *Thorn* disappeared into the night.

On board the *Thorn,* the slaver's men had confined Grover in his cabin. Grover attempted to leave but was met by Gomez with a dirk in his hand and a group of Spanish seamen carrying pistols and cutlasses. Gomez warned Grover they would kill him if he tried to come on deck again. Then Gomez set a course for Cuba.

The *Capital* arrived at the wreck site the next morning and, together with the *General Geddes,* began salvaging sails, rigging, guns, and other items of value from the *Guerrero.* The *Surprize,* having survived the night under the protection of *General Geddes'* armed crew, got underway at eight o'clock. As she was about to pass the *Nimble,* Holland hailed her and asked where she was headed. Someone on the *Surprize* replied "Key West." But in his deposition, Sanderson said he intended to anchor by the *Nimble* for protection. Sanderson also stated that the Spaniards had offered him two doubloons for each African he would land in Cuba. In any event, Holland told Sanderson to anchor immediately or he would fire. When Sanderson appeared to be slow in coming to anchor, Holland had his men fire three musket shots.

Once the *Surprize* was anchored, a British officer and several seamen went aboard her and sent all the Spaniards except two over to the *Nimble*. With the officer and four of his men remaining on board to guard the Spaniards, the *Surprize* got under way and sailed for Key West.

An hour later, an officer from the *Nimble* came aboard the *General Geddes* and asked Morrison to tow the *Nimble* to Key Tavernier to get a replacement rudder from a wreck known to be there. The officer assured Morrison that the British government would pay him generously for the service–at least three times as much as he would get by continuing to salvage goods from the *Guerrero*. Morrison agreed to help but said it would be better and faster to remove the rudder from the wrecked brig and have two of his crewmen who were skilled carpenters fit it to the *Nimble*.

For the rest of that day and most of the next, divers and carpenters from the *General Geddes* worked at removing the rudder from the *Guerrero,* altering it to fit, and installing it at the *Nimble*'s stern. During that time, seamen from the *Capital* and the *Nimble* continued salvaging boats, sails, rigging, guns, furnishings, and other materials from the wrecked brig. On the morning of December 23, three days after she had struck the reef, the *Nimble* got under way with Morrison serving as pilot and arrived safely at Key West the following night

The Spanish slavers in control of the *Thorn* and the *Florida* forced them to sail to Santa Cruz, Cuba, arriving on December 22. On arrival, the Spaniards herded the 398 Africans, worth nearly $120,000, ashore to be sold into slavery. They warned Grover and Packer not to attempt to leave port until the following day. For unknown reasons, all of *Thorn*'s crew, except the mate, the pilot, and one seaman, deserted that night, taking the schooner's sole remaining boat with them. The next morning, with some of the *Florida*'s men assisting the short-handed crew of the *Thorn,* the two vessels returned to Key West.

The *Surprize* had arrived in Key West on December 22 and delivered her 120 Africans, one having died on the way, to the collector of customs. He, in turn, placed them in the custody of the U.S. Marshall. Holland protested that the slaves should remain in his custody because the *Guerrero* had surrendered to him.

The captains of the four wrecking vessels asked Holland if he would agree to have their salvage claim settled by arbitration, then the only available means in Key West. Holland acknowledged that the wreckers had furnished valuable services. But having learned that the arbitrators would be either owners, part owners, or interested in some other way in the wrecking vessels, he refused to submit to their decision. Saying he would only agree to settlement by a competent United States tribunal, he got the *Nimble* under way and sailed out of the harbor on December 27. So far as is known, the British government never paid a salvage award for the wreckers' aid to the *Nimble*. The wreckers' only compensation for their efforts were the proceeds from the sale of the materials they had recovered from the *Guerrero*.

During the time the Africans were held in Key West, rumors arose that a Cuban expedition was forming to come and take them by force. The citizens mounted cannons in the streets to defend the town. Other locals made unsuccessful attempts to get possession of some of the Africans by stealth or by bribery. After three months, the Africans were transported to St. Augustine and, a year later, as a result of special legislation sponsored by President Adams, began their journey back to Africa. The surviving Africans, only ninety-one in number, finally reached Liberia on March 4, 1830.

Chapter 8

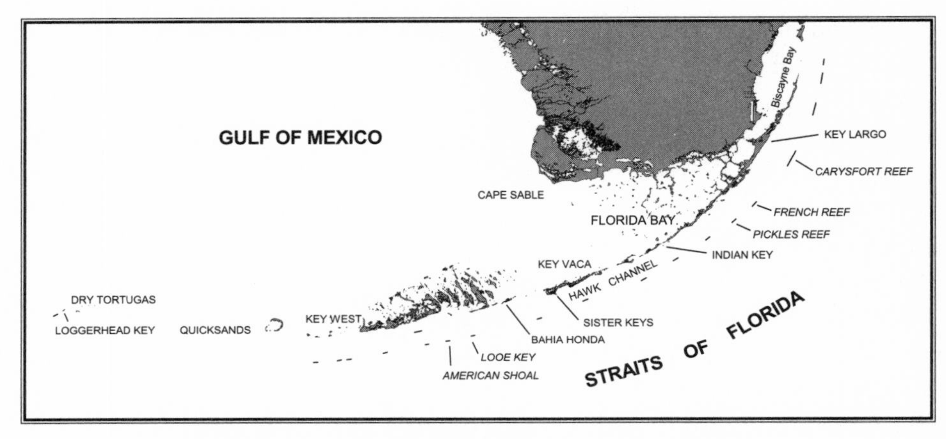

The Florida Keys and the Florida Reef (drawing by Erich Mueller)

NEGLIGENCE, MISCONDUCT, AND FRAUD

Negligence

John Burrows, captain of the fishing smack *Francisco,* stood before Judge Marvin anxiously waiting to hear what salvage award he would receive. Three days earlier, on September 5, 1849, he had gone to the aid of the ship *Allegheny,* aground in the Dry Tortugas, in consort with the wrecking sloop *George Eldridge.* Before either of the wreckers arrived, the master of the *Allegheny,* in an attempt to get his ship off by himself, had ordered his crew to throw overboard the deck load of cart wheels and cart bodies.

The wrecking crews offloaded part of the ship's cargo and heaved her afloat. That afternoon, the *Allegheny* set sail for Key West, accompanied by the *George Eldridge.* The *Francisco* remained behind to recover the cargo thrown overboard. With the aid of their diver, the *Francisco*'s crew pulled up nine cart wheels and one cart body. There were still ten cart wheels and another cart body on the bottom, but the diver was exhausted and had injured himself. Burrows decided his diver had done enough and sailed for Key West, where he delivered the cart wheels and cart body to the custody of the court.

Burrows could hardly believe his ears as the judge, reading his decree, said, "Burrows then became impatient and sailed for Key West leaving behind the [ten] cartwheels and perhaps a cart body that might have been obtained if a little more energy, patience, and perseverance had been used. I have heard Burrow's excuses and explanations for not obtaining those ten wheels and they are entirely unsatisfactory to my mind. Under the circumstances he should have obtained them and brought them here. For his neglect and omission, $100 must be deducted from the smack's share of the salvage and forfeited to the ship unless he shall deliver the ten wheels to the ship's consignee in this place, free of charge, within ten days."

It was not enough that a wrecker saved the ship or its cargo if, in the process, he failed to use good judgment, employ appropriate methods, have proper equipment available, or do everything that could have been done. Judge Marvin, in his book *The Law of Wreck and Salvage,* wrote: "If in consequence of neglect or want of skill in sounding out channels, carrying out anchors, or navigating the vessel, or from any other omission of proper care

It was not enough that a wrecker saved a ship or its cargo; there were other considerations as well. (*Scribner's Magazine*, Vol. III, January–June 1888, p. 257. From the collections of The Mariners' Museum, Newport News, Virginia)

or skill, the salvors incur unnecessary delay in extricating the vessel from its perilous situation, or get it ashore a second time, their salvage ought to be reduced in proportion to the degree of negligence, or the want of skill; and, where the negligence is gross or willful, it should be wholly forfeited."

On occasion, masters of wrecked ships, after they were heaved afloat, would ask wrecking captains to pilot them to Key West, particularly if they were sailing inside the reef. Most wrecking captains were not licensed pilots, but the court considered they were qualified to act as such given their knowledge of the waters along the reef. Two wrecking captains in succession told the master of a schooner surrounded by shoals that they were not pilots and refused to guide the schooner clear. In attempting to negotiate the shoals without their help, the schooner went aground. The judge reduced the wreckers' salvage award to $100, saying they should have piloted the schooner out of the shoal water when they first boarded her.

If a wrecking captain did agree to pilot and then ran the ship aground unintentionally, he could expect to have his salvage award reduced. The ship *Tennessee,* sailing from Bordeaux to New Orleans, struck Carysfort Reef in May 1839. The ship ground across the reef, floated free, and anchored in three fathoms of water, still surrounded by coral heads. Several wrecking vessels arrived shortly after daybreak. The *Tennessee*'s master asked them to pilot him out of the shoal waters. The first wrecking captain refused, saying he was not well. The next captain said he would try, but only if the ship's master would not hold him responsible if he put the ship aground.

With a mate in a boat sounding ahead to find the deepest water, the *Tennessee* got under way. An hour and a half later, she grounded, came off, then grounded again and remained fast. The wreckers carried out anchors, offloaded cargo, and finally heaved the ship afloat. The next day, with a different wrecking captain as pilot, the *Tennessee* went aground again. The crew hauled the sails aback to catch the wind from the other side; the ship came free and was anchored. On the third day, the pilot steered the ship across the reef and reached Key West without further incident.

In the subsequent court case, the *Tennessee*'s master asked the judge to consider that all the damage to his ship took place while she was in the hands of the wreckers. Judge Marvin seemed to agree, saying, "The extraordinary facts and circumstances present to my mind a singular alternative, that either some strange and unaccounted fatality, some evil doom must have visited upon this ship and cargo or else that the conduct of the wreckers has not been such in regard to them as to entitle them to salvage; but on the contrary is highly culpable and reprehensible." Based on this opinion, the judge decreed a reduced salvage award of twenty-five percent.

In another case, the captain of a fishing smack accepted a fee of $100 to pilot a brig to Key West inside the reef and then ran her aground. The judge agreed that he had not done it deliberately but still denied him any salvage award.

Failure to take soundings or to take sufficient soundings before attempting to haul a grounded ship off the reef was cause for a reduction in the salvage award. Having failed to sound around the ship *Ashburton,* aground on American Shoals in 1855, the wreckers heaved her off only to have her go aground on another ridge. Judge Marvin reduced their award from fifteen to eleven percent.

Eight wrecking vessels plus twenty-eight men hired from small fishing boats got the ship *Diadem* off the reef at Looe Key in three days. Nevertheless, the master of the *Diadem* criticized the wreckers for improperly rigging the bridle to the anchor and for failing to have an adequate supply of anchors, hawsers, and chains on board their vessels. Judge Marvin gave his opinion that the wreckers could have gotten the ship off a day earlier had it not been for their negligence, carelessness, and gross errors of judgment. He cut their salvage award in half.

Not only did the wreckers have to save the cargo, they had to also preserve it from being damaged, lost, or stolen while it was in their hands. The wrecking sloop *Elisha Beckwith* was one of eleven wrecking vessels involved in salvaging the cargo of the ship *Mulhouse,* lost on the Quicksands west of the Marquesas Keys in 1859. Included in the cargo were kegs containing $25,500 worth of specie (coins). The *Beckwith*'s crew took the kegs and the ship's master on board and proceeded to Key West. During the night after the *Beckwith*'s arrival, one of her crewmen, aided by confederates from shore, stole one of the kegs containing $5,000 in specie and dropped it over the side, intending to recover it at a later time. When the theft was discovered the next day, three divers located the keg and raised it. For failing to guard the specie, the captain of the *Elisha Beckwith* forfeited his share of the salvage award.

Even when none of their own crewmen were involved in theft, the wreckers did not escape punishment. The small schooner *Independent,* not a full-time wrecker, and the U.S. Light House Service schooner *Florida* went to the aid of the brig *Ben Cushing,* ashore and bilged on French Reef in 1862. They took the crew and their personal baggage off and carried them to Key West. The wreckers were unaware that some of the brig's crewmen had broken open cases of cigars, concealed the cigars in their sea chests and bags, and smuggled them ashore at Key West. Judge Marvin reduced the salvage award to the *Independent* because her crew did not use due diligence to detect, inquire into, and expose the theft.

Misconduct

The wrecking crews faced temptation every time they descended into a ship's hold to remove cargo. Rich silks, ready-made clothing, chinaware, cigars, wine, and liquors were just a few of the many valuable goods that passed through their hands and would be relatively easy to secrete. That very few of the wreckers succumbed to such temptations is testimony to

Wrecking crews faced temptation every time they descended into a ship's hold to remove cargo. (sketch by S. G. W. Benjamin in *Harper's Weekly*, Oct. 19, 1878, courtesy of Florida State Archives)

their basic honesty. In 360 wrecking court cases decided between 1830 and 1861, only four wreckers were penalized for minor thefts of cargo.

In 1836, Captains Joseph Bethel, Thomas Johnston, and John Mott forfeited their salvage awards for ordering their crewmen to take some sugar and coffee from the wreck of the *Dorothea Foster* and put it on board their wrecking vessels.

A more serious charge was levied against the captain of the sloop *Empire* in 1848. The ship *Quebec* went ashore on Carysfort Reef in January. Her crew threw a large quantity of cargo overboard, after which they were able to heave her afloat and continue on the voyage. A number of wrecking and fishing vessels picked up floating items, and their divers retrieved other items from the bottom. After delivering the goods to the custody of the court in Key West, the judge awarded them sixty percent of the value of the items they had recovered. But the insurance agent for the *Quebec*'s cargo charged that Thomas Bennett, captain of the *Empire,* had failed to deliver some coats, pantaloons, hats, paintings, and other goods that he had recovered. Bennett admitted that he had picked up some items and distributed them to his crew. He also admitted that he had stored some rocking chairs and oil paintings in a vacant house on Key Largo, from which they were later stolen. He maintained that these items did not come from the *Quebec* and that he was not aware that items found floating at sea were within the jurisdiction of the court. Judge Marvin ruled that ignorance of the law was no excuse and ordered Bennett's salvage award forfeited and his license revoked.

On a few occasions, masters of wrecked ships reported that wrecking crewmen had broken into the ship's liquor stores and become intoxicated. If the report was substantiated, the judge would order that all or a portion of the crewmen's shares be forfeited. Surprisingly, in 360 pre–Civil War wrecking court cases, fewer than a dozen seamen lost shares as a result of intoxication.

Further evidence of the strict code of conduct enforced on wrecking captains is found in the cases of the barks *Yucatan* and *Howard* and the brig *Flora.* Joseph Stickney, captain of the schooner *Governor Bennet,* arrived late at the wreck of the bark *Yucatan* and was not admitted to the consortship by the wreck master. Desperate for a share of the spoils, and against the express orders of the bark's master and the wreck master, he had his diver retrieve a cotton bale that had fallen overboard. The judge denied his libel for salvage on the bale.

When Frederick Fresca, captain of the sloop *Globe,* came aboard the bark *Howard* ashore on Sister Key Shoals off Key Vaca in 1838, the master of the bark asked him if his wrecking crewmen would assist the ship's crew in kedging the ship off. Fresca replied that his men could assist if they wanted to do so. The *Globe's* crew said they would not help unless the master of the bark gave up his ship (turned over control) to their captain. Three more wrecking vessels arrived on the scene and also refused to help unless the bark's master gave up his ship to them. The bark's crew continued their efforts to heave the ship afloat without success. The next day, the bark's master agreed to turn over the salvage operation to the wreckers. The wreckers offloaded cargo, heaved the bark off, and with twenty-three men at the pumps, got her to Key West. Judge Marvin reprimanded Captain Fresca and the other captains for not directing their men to help the bark's crew when they were first asked. He ordered Fresca to forfeit all his shares of the salvage award and the other three captains to forfeit one share each.

The brig *Flora* was ashore on Sister Key in 1842, and the wrecking sloop *Westpoint* was alongside offloading. John Curry, in the wrecking schooner *Rome,* arrived on the scene and asked to be allowed to participate in the salvage operation. The master of the *Flora* replied that they were unloading as fast as possible and that no additional assistance was needed. Curry offered to pay the master well if he would let the *Rome* come alongside and threatened to tell the court if he was not allowed to. The master then agreed to let the *Rome* offload cargo. In court, Judge Marvin ruled that Curry's threat to tell the court if his offer was refused was improper conduct. He ordered Curry to forfeit half of his three shares but not more since this was his first offense.

Fraud

Not all the wrecks on the Florida Reef were accidents. Either in league with the owners for a share of the insurance money or in collusion with the wreckers for a share of the salvage money, ship masters would sometimes deliberately run their vessels ashore, and even sometimes drill holes in the hull to ensure that the wreckers could not save them. If collusion with a wrecker was proven, the wrecker, of course, lost his license. But as the following examples show, collusion was very difficult to prove.

The brig *Francis Ashby* sprung a leak when about twenty miles from Key West and hoisted her colors upside down at half-mast as a distress signal. The wrecking sloop *George Eldridge* came to her assistance and piloted her across the reef into Hawk Channel. The brig's pumps would not work because they were clogged with coffee, so the captain of the *Eldridge* advised the brig's master to run her aground on Loggerhead Key off Cudjoe Key. Three more wreckers arrived on the scene, and all went to work to offload cargo. As they did so, the leak decreased, but by the next morning, it had mysteriously increased. Despite this, the wreckers managed to get the brig afloat and bring her safely to Key West. Upon arrival, divers inspected the underwater hull and found that six auger holes had been drilled in the bottom. Whether one of the brig's crew or one of the wreckers had drilled them was never discovered. Judge Marvin ruled that since two of the wreckers were alongside the brig the night the holes were drilled and the other two wreckers were anchored nearby, none of the wreckers would receive a salvage award. He did, however, allow them to recover their costs. On appeal, his decision was upheld for all but one of the wreckers, the smallest, which somehow proved that her crew could not have been responsible.

The story of the brig *Josephine,* stranded on Carysfort Reef in 1850, is a complex one. There are two versions, one as told by the master of the brig and one as related by the wreckers.

The master said that after striking the reef, the brig crossed over it and anchored in deep water. A pilot who happened to be nearby because of the construction of Carysfort Reef Lighthouse came aboard and, after some delay waiting for a favorable wind, got the brig under way and promptly ran her aground. In court, the master claimed that the pilot deliberately grounded the brig in order to give the two wreckers he was in league with the opportunity to obtain a salvage award. He also reported that after the brig floated free, the two wreckers continued to take off cargo unnecessarily. At this point, the master discharged the first two wreckers and obtained

American steamship *General Meade* went ashore on reef in September 1866 and was gotten off by seven wrecking vessels. Master agreed to pay wreckers $25,000, then took kickback of $10,000 (see Chapter 10). (from the collections of The Mariners' Museum, Newport News, Virginia)

the services of a third wrecker to kedge the brig clear of the reef. He further charged that the first two wrecking captains offered his supercargo (cargo owner's representative) a bribe to let them take cargo out.

In their libel, the two wrecking captains claimed that the supercargo demanded that they pay him and the master a sum of money to allow the brig to become a total wreck, after which they could remove all the cargo to obtain a maximum salvage award. They alleged that when they refused his demand, they were dismissed.

The judge was unable to determine which side was telling the truth and suspected that both were guilty of misconduct. Because the first two wreckers had offloaded cargo unnecessarily, he decreed there would be no salvage award. Despite his suspicions of fraudulent conduct on the part of the brig's master and supercargo, in the absence of any proof, he restored the cargo to the brig.

When, in May 1854, the master of the bark *Byron* went aground for the third time in his attempts to get free of Carysfort Reef, he reluctantly accepted the services of the seven wreckers standing by. The wreckers carried out an anchor ahead, offloaded a large portion of the cargo, and eventually heaved the bark free. After studying the testimony of the wreckers and the bark's master carefully and noting that the shoal could be seen, the judge realized that the anchor should have been carried out astern. He commented, "There is no possible way of accounting for their carrying it out ahead but by supposing that they desired to keep this vessel on the reef and by lightening her to a considerable extent and more than was necessary make out an artificial and fabricated case of meritorious salvage services and impose it on the court as genuine. . . ." He also suspected that the master of the bark might have deliberately overlooked what was going on, or, if not, was guilty of gross neglect of his duty. Judge Marvin ordered the wreckers' salvage claims forfeited but did allow them to recover their costs since they had gotten the bark off the reef.

The Infamous Jacob Housman

Whether he deserved it or not, during the 1820s and 1830s, Capt. Jacob Housman earned the reputation of being the most unprincipled, dishonest wrecking captain on the reef. As a young man, he learned about the wrecking business firsthand when he ran a small schooner he had "borrowed" from his father up on the Florida Reef. Forced to put into Key West for repairs, he soon realized that wrecking offered the perfect outlet for his adventurous, ambitious nature. Beginning his wrecking operations sometime in the early 1820s, he soon became frustrated by the tight control over every aspect of the business exercised by the merchants of Key West. They owned all the wharves, warehouses, and ship repair facilities and many of the wrecking vessels, and were often the political leaders of the community. By means of gentlemen's agreements among themselves, they were able to reap most of the wrecking profits.

Relations between Housman and the Key West merchants gradually deteriorated and finally reached a head when, in 1825, Fielding A. Browne, a leading merchant, accused Housman of committing "a most villainous act." Browne, then serving as acting collector of customs, charged that Housman had robbed a French brig, the *Revenge*, which he found cast ashore and abandoned on the reef. In a letter to the captain of the revenue cutter *Florida,* he wrote that Housman had defied the civil and military authorities at Key West and was on his way to Charleston to dispose of the cargo. He asked the cutter captain to pursue Housman, recover the property taken from the brig, and bring Housman to justice. But the captain had other orders and could not comply.

Browne's letter was subsequently published in a New York newspaper and came to Housman's attention. In response, Housman wrote a letter to the public, which was also published. In it he said that Browne's accusations were libel. He claimed that he had removed the brig's cargo at the master's request and had had written authority to do so. He stated that he had then carried the cargo to St. Augustine, where the circumstances were investigated by the admiralty court of East Florida and he was awarded a portion of the cargo for his salvage efforts.

Housman concluded his denial of Browne's charges by saying, "I shall take another occasion to lay before the public a history of the *impartial* and *disinterested* conduct of the gentlemen of many avocations at Key West, in their disposal of property falling under their control, and it will then be fairly understood, whether there was most wisdom or folly in my giving a preference to a decision at St. Augustine over Key West."

What Housman did not say in his letter was that, on arrival in St. Augustine, he had first submitted his salvage claim to a five-man jury as allowed by the territorial law on wrecking, and the jury had awarded him ninety-five percent of the value of the cargo. The French consul, who happened to be in St. Augustine at the time, considered the award outrageous and sued in superior court to have it revoked. In the record of the court proceedings, there are some significant discrepancies between Housman's account of what happened and the events as summarized by the judge. According to the judge's narrative, Housman found the brig deserted and removed what cargo he was able to before heavy weather drove him off. Sometime later, Housman came across the brig's boat, with the captain and crew on board, making its way toward Key West. They were unable to converse because neither Housman nor any of his crew could speak French, and, apparently, the Frenchmen could not speak English. Based on this account, it is difficult to understand how Housman could have obtained written authorization to remove the cargo before he had even met the captain and, when he did, could not converse with him.

Nevertheless, the judge found no evidence "to sustain the slightest imputation of unfairness or unkindness on the part of the salvor to the crew of the wreck" and awarded Housman two-thirds of the value of the cargo he had saved. The judge also pronounced the territorial wrecking law under which Housman had been awarded ninety-five percent invalid.

Three years later, another newspaper story did further damage to Housman's reputation by accusing him of paying a bribe to the master of the wrecked brig *Vigilant.* After striking the reef near Key Vaca, the brig had managed to get afloat again but was surrounded by shoal water. A local pilot, Daniel Mellus, together with another man, went to her assistance and piloted her to a safe anchorage at Key Vaca. At this point, Housman appeared on the scene in his wrecking sloop, *Sarah Isabella.* According to Mellus, Housman demanded a share in the salvage award and threatened to take the brig by force if he was refused. Housman then made a deal with the brig's master to pilot the brig to Key West for seventy-five percent of the value of the cargo, which included $32,000 in specie. According to the newspaper account, the offer was made "with the understanding that Housman would return part of the money to the Captain for Himself." The article noted that this information was communicated by "a most respectable authority who had evidence to support it."

The *Vigilant* and her cargo were sold at Key West. Housman received $27,000 and Mellus received only $3,000. Mellus sued the master for $6,000. The master placed $6,000 on deposit in Key West, boarded Housman's sloop, and the two men departed in the night, presumably for Charleston. No information has been found as to why Mellus specified the sum of $6,000 or whether or not he ever received it. A little less than a year later, Mellus sued Housman for a share of the $27,000, but the outcome of that case is also unknown.

In the meantime, Housman had been slowly building up his fortune and searching for a place to escape the control of the "merchants of many avocations" at Key West. He found it on a tiny island named Indian Key, seventy miles from Key West off Lower Matecumbe Key. Since 1824, a store there had catered to the needs of the wreckers, and, by 1829, there were a half dozen families on the island. It was a popular rendezvous for the wreckers because it was near the part of the reef that attracted the most wrecks. Not only could they obtain supplies and provisions for their vessels, they could also amuse themselves at the nine-pin bowling alley and billiard table in the hotel.

By 1830, Housman had accumulated enough money to purchase another small wrecking sloop, the *Martha Jane*, and to buy a house on Indian Key. He also had the misfortune to run afoul of the collector of customs at Key West. According to the story he presented to Judge Webb in superior court, he had gone to the aid of the British brig *Peter Ellis,* ashore on the reef, gotten her off, and brought her to Key West. While he was alongside the brig offloading cargo, the brig's cook deserted, and the master asked Housman to allow his crew to eat on board the *Sarah Isabella.* To compensate for the food his men had eaten, the brig's master had his crew transfer several barrels of beef and bread to the *Sarah Isabella.* He also presented Housman with several old sails by way of appreciation.

When the *Sarah Isabella* arrived in Key West, the collector of customs seized the barrels and sails for violation of revenue laws, that is, they had been brought into the U.S. from a foreign country without payment of duty. The collector also seized an anchor and anchor chain that he found on board. Housman claimed that he found the anchor and chain lying on the bottom and there was no indication of to whom they belonged. Housman sued in superior court to recover the items, but lost and was required to pay court costs.

Whenever possible, Housman avoided pursuing his claim for salvage in the superior court. Instead, he convinced the master of the *Peter Ellis* to agree to have the claim settled by arbitration. Two arbitrators awarded Housman a generous sixty-two percent of the net worth of the vessel and cargo. Benjamin Strobel, a Key West physician and newspaper editor at the time, later insinuated that Housman had offered a bribe to the brig's master to get him to agree to arbitration. Strobel put it this way: "What amount the captain received on his own account, I never learned."

In 1831, Housman and another wrecking captain hauled a brig, the *Halcyon,* off the reef and brought her to Key West. With his usual persuasive power, Housman got the master to agree to arbitration of the salvage claim. Two "disinterested persons" awarded the salvors fifty-six percent of the value of the brig and cargo. When the agent of the brig's owners learned of the award, he sued in the superior court to have the award reduced. Judge

Webb was of the opinion that both sides had overstated the facts of the case. As far as he was concerned, it was a routine salvage operation. The wreckers were not exposed to any great hazard as they claimed and the ship was not in danger of being lost. He reduced the salvors' award to twenty-five percent but did not find any fault with Housman's conduct.

Proceeding with his plan to make Indian Key his own personal empire, Housman in 1831 purchased the store, the two-story house that served as a hotel, and the rights to a claim of ownership of the entire island. For all this he paid $5,000.

Two years later, despite his best efforts to avoid the place, he was in court again. The schooner *North Carolina,* loaded with 366 bales of cotton, had gone ashore on Pickles Reef. It was gotten off by the schooner *Hyder Ally* and taken to Indian Key. The *Sarah Isabella* and the *Brilliant* were consorted with the *Hyder Ally* but took no part in the salvage operation. After the *North Carolina* was safely moored at Indian Key, Housman conferred with the master. Without explaining to the master that he already stood to receive a share of the salvage award, he talked the master into submitting the claim to arbitration at Indian Key. He also got the master to appoint him as his business agent.

The two arbitrators, both of them residents of Indian Key, awarded the salvors thirty-five percent of the value of the schooner and its cargo, which they appraised at $8,940. They appraised the cotton, which had sold for $30 a bale at Apalachicola, at $20 a bale. The master of the *North Carolina* paid the award with 122 bales of cotton, $100 cash, and a draft for $600. Housman received one-third of the award plus five percent for his role as business agent. He then sailed off to Charleston, where he was able to sell fifty bales of the cotton at $50 a bale.

When the agent of the cargo's consignees received news of the transactions at Indian Key, he sued Housman and the other two salvors in superior court at Key West. Judge Webb found that the agreement between Housman and the *North Carolina's* master was fraudulent and ordered Housman to return the seventy-two bales of cotton still in storage at Indian Key. Housman appealed to the Territorial Court of Appeals and, failing to win there, to the U.S. Supreme Court. In 1841, the Supreme Court decided that the "transactions at Indian Key were evidently in bad faith," and decreed "that the salvors, by their conduct, have forfeited all claim to compensation, even for the service actually rendered."

Despite this setback, Housman's fortunes continued to improve. His store was doing a booming business, not only with the wreckers, but also with the settlers on Biscayne Bay and Key Vaca and with the natives on the southern mainland. He purchased another wrecking schooner but poured most of his money into improving his little eleven-acre tropical commercial empire. With slave labor, he laid out streets and a town square and built wharves, a large warehouse, houses, and shops for the ships' carpenters, sailmakers, and a blacksmith. He also imported large shipments of fertile soil and planted fruit trees, coconut palms, and gardens.

One key to Housman's success was his hold over the wreckers, fishermen, and turtlers who patronized his store. He would let them buy on credit and then use their indebtedness to get them to do him favors. One of these favors was to give him an exclusive report of any wreck they sighted, even if it meant bypassing a wrecking vessel much nearer the scene.

As a further step to freeing himself from having to deal with his enemies–the merchants, lawyers, and political leaders of Key West–Housman in 1835 submitted a petition to the Territorial Legislative Council asking that Monroe County be split into two counties with the boundary line at Bahia Honda. His petition was granted, and the new county, named Dade, included all the middle and upper Keys as well as a large section of the mainland. Indian Key was made the temporary county seat, and Housman built a courthouse to house the county judge, who also happened to be his personal attorney.

But just when everything seemed to be going Housman's way, the Seminole Indians, in December 1835, went on the warpath, and Housman's empire began to disintegrate. Almost immediately, settlers deserted the southern mainland and Key Vaca. With their departure, business at the store on Indian Key fell off precipitously.

One year later, Housman's conduct in another wrecking operation caused further damage to his reputation and finances. The ship *Ajax* ran up on Carysfort Reef and bilged in November 1836. The weather was rough, but four wreckers managed to remove the ninety passengers and their baggage safely. They took some of the cargo off by boat before heavy seas drove them away. Later the wrecking vessels *Van Buren, Caroline, Thistle, Fair American,* and *Sarah Isabella* arrived and salvaged more cargo by having divers retrieve it from the flooded hold. Housman owned the *Thistle, Fair American,* and *Sarah Isabella* and was on board and acting as captain of the *Sarah Isabella.*

As she was getting under way from alongside the wreck, the *Thistle* struck the stock of the ship's anchor lying on the bottom, stove a hole in her hull, and sank. The *Fair American* rescued her crew, but the *Thistle* was a total loss.

Because the first four wreckers submitted their libels in the superior court at Key West, Housman was forced to follow suit. In response to Housman's libel, the master of the *Ajax* charged that the *Fair American* had stopped at Indian Key before returning to Key West. He claimed that she had remained there an unreasonable length of time, which resulted in unnecessary deterioration of the wet clothing, linens, silks, and cottons that she had loaded. He further charged that the *Fair American* had failed to deliver $2,000 worth of clothing, linens, silks, and cottons to Key West. He also accused Housman of taking a coil of new rope, two anchor stoppers, and other articles from the wreck and failing to deliver them to Key West.

In response to the charges, Housman stated that the *Fair American* had been forced to put into Indian Key because, with the *Thistle*'s crew on board, she had run short of provisions and water. Further delay occurred when, while at anchor, she swung onto a shoal bank and was unable to get off until the next high tide. Despite this, she arrived at Key West just three days after leaving the wreck and delivered the entire lot of clothing, linens, silks, and cottons at the public wharf.

Housman denied that he had failed to deliver any of the articles he had taken from the wreck of the *Ajax* to Key West. As for the coil of rope, he said that it had been placed aboard the *Thistle* and was lost when she sank.

Judge Webb decreed a salvage award of thirty-five percent of the net amount realized from the sale of the salvaged goods. But apparently he did not believe Housman's explanation for the *Fair American*'s stop at Indian Key or the missing cloth and coil of rope. He ordered that Housman and the captain of the *Fair American* forfeit their "individual" shares. It is not clear whether this meant that Housman also lost the shares due him as owner of both vessels. Again, Housman appealed the judgement to the Territorial Court of Appeals, which upheld the decision against him.

The *Ajax* was the last wrecking operation in which Housman was directly involved that there is any official record of. A story written by a journalist in 1859, twenty-one years after the event, seems to indicate that Housman's wrecking license was revoked by Judge Webb as a result of his conduct in the *Ajax* incident, but the story is suspect because it contains numerous errors of fact. No official record of revocation of Housman's license has yet been found.

Although Housman had managed to sever political ties with Key West, he was still obliged to deliver wrecked goods there because Indian Key was not a port of entry. In 1836, 1838, and 1839, Housman submitted petitions to Congress to make Indian Key a port of entry. Thirty-seven wrecking captains signed a memorial against Housman's 1839 petition, saying, "We know of no such instances [of cargoes being lost between Indian Key and Key West]; nor do we know of any recent instances of cargoes being landed at Indian Key, except by the proprietor of that island [Housman]; and we are constrained to say, that all he has thus landed has never been fully accounted for." Congress denied all Housman's petitions largely because of unfavorable testimony such as this.

For reasons that are not completely clear, Housman's finances went into a steady decline after the start of the Second Seminole War. The flight of settlers from the mainland and Key Vaca greatly reduced the income from his store. He also spent a considerable sum of money arming and paying a small militia company to guard the island. He still owned four wrecking schooners, but whether or not they were paying their way is not known. In any event, by March 1840, he was out of money and forced to mortgage the entire island and all his buildings, estimated to be worth $144,000, to two Charleston men for $14,283.

The final blow to his downhill slide came on August 7, 1840, when a Seminole war party raided the island, killed five residents, and left it a smoking ruin. Nine months later, Housman was dead, reportedly killed in an accident while working as a seaman on a wrecking vessel.

Whether Housman's bad reputation was entirely his own fault or unfairly enlarged by his enemies in Key West is a question that may never be answered. But there is no question that he did more to give the wreckers of the Florida Reef a bad name than did any other wrecking captain.

Chapter 9

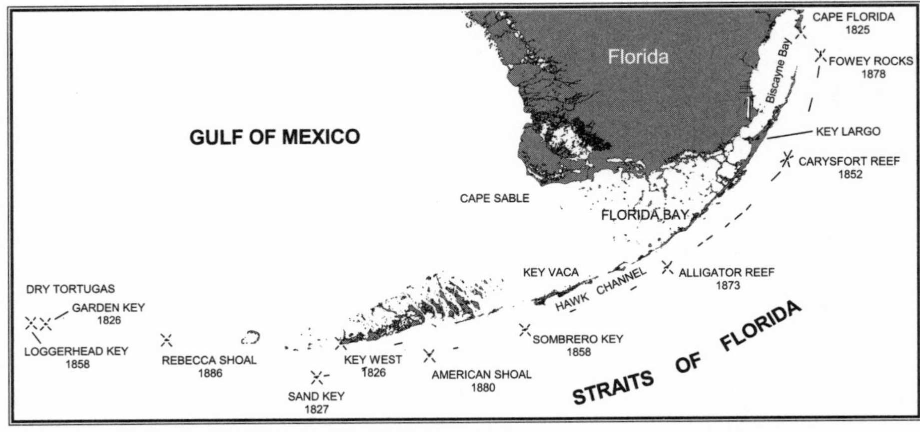

Lighthouses on the reef with dates first lighted (drawing by Erich Mueller)

THOSE DAMN LIGHTS!

Wrecking Spurs Key West Growth

Fueled by the income from wrecking and its allied pursuits, Key West grew and prospered during the decades preceding the Civil War. Jefferson Browne, chronicler of Key West history, wrote, "Prior to 1860, Key West was much the most important city in Florida." Walter C. Maloney, a respected civic leader, stated in a speech delivered in 1876, "We claim for Key West that it is the Commercial Emporium of the State of Florida."

Other maritime industries, particularly fishing and turtling, contributed much to the city's growth. In 1849, the harvesting and marketing of natural sponges began, creating an industry that would eventually supplant wrecking in economic importance.

Military construction projects plus supplies and services for military personnel stationed in Key West provided further boosts to the city's economic growth. Construction of Fort Taylor, guarding the main entrance channel to the port, began in 1845. The following year, work began on Fort Jefferson in the Dry Tortugas, at the western entrance to the Straits of Florida. Called America's Gibraltar, it was the largest brick fortification in the United States. Work on both forts continued through the Civil War years. Two infantry companies arrived in Key West in 1831 and moved into permanent barracks constructed for them on the north side of the island in 1844. Construction of the first permanent navy buildings, a storehouse, and a coaling facility was authorized in 1852, but they were not completed until the Civil War years.

Lighting the Reef

The 1850s were the peak years for the wrecking industry. At the same time, however, developments such as the construction of lighthouses and surveys of the reef were taking place that would begin a gradual decline of and, eventually, an end to the days of sailing wrecking vessels patrolling the reef.

One of the first to recognize the need for lighthouses along the Florida Reef was Lt. Matthew C. Perry, USN, who commanded the U.S. Schooner *Shark* and took possession of Key West for the United States in March 1822. In a letter to the secretary of the navy reporting on his survey of the island, he wrote, "Numberless are the Vessels, and lives, that have been lost on this treacherous Coast, so common are Ship Wrecks in this neighborhood, that many Vessels are employed solely for the purpose of rescueing [sic] property from destruction, of which they receive a very large share as salvage. . . . The great number of vessels that daily pass through the Gulf of Florida [Straits of Florida], to and from Ports of Cuba, Jamaica and the Spanish Main renders the erection of Light Houses, not only as an act of justice on the part of our Government, But humanity and a regard to the safety of the lives and fortunes of our citizens seriously demand so desirable a measure."

Lieutenant Perry recommended lights be placed at four locations: at Cape Florida on the southern point of Key Biscayne, abreast Key Largo, on Sand Key near the entrance to Key West, and in the Dry Tortugas. Evidently someone in Washington took note of his recommendations. Between 1825 and 1827, the government authorized construction of lighthouses at Cape Florida, Key West, Sand Key, and Garden Key in the Dry Tortugas. In addition, a lightship was anchored on Carysfort Reef off Key Largo in 1826.

Despite these early lights, ships continued to pile up on the reef in ever-increasing numbers, much to the delight of the wreckers. Often masters of ships that went aground would claim that the lights were dim or not showing. They complained most about the lighthouse at the Dry Tortugas and the lightship at Carysfort Reef. Several ship masters said the light at the Dry Tortugas was so dim they thought they were ten miles away from it when they ran aground two or three miles away. The captain of the *Isabel,* a mail-passenger-freight steamer making twice-monthly runs between Key West and Charleston, called the Carysfort lightship "a poor thing . . . cannot depend on it at all."

The early lighthouses and lightships not only received much criticism over the dependability of their lights but also suffered one disaster after another. A storm drove the first lightship for Carysfort Reef, the *Caesar,* ashore as she was on her way south in 1825. This delayed her arrival on station for a year. After being on station for only five years, the *Caesar*

Lightship *Florida* stationed at Carysfort Reef in 1831. Seminole Indians lying in ambush on Key Largo killed the captain and one crewman in 1837. (drawing by James Lloyd)

was revealed to be a mass of dry rot and fungus. The lightship *Florida,* built to replace her, took station at Carysfort in 1831.

When the Second Seminole War began in 1836, the settlers on the south Florida mainland fled to Key West. The Cape Florida Lighthouse was abandoned for a short period and then manned again. In July of that year, a band of Seminoles attacked the lighthouse, setting the interior on fire, wounding the keeper, and killing his assistant. Ten years passed before the lighthouse was rebuilt and relighted. The lightship *Florida* then became the closest white man's outpost to hostile territory. In June 1837, the captain and four of his crew went ashore on Key Largo to gather stovewood. A party of Indians, lying in ambush, fired at them, killing the captain and one of his crewmen. The other three seamen, two of them wounded, managed to escape in their boat before the Indians could fire again.

Indians were not the only peril lighthouse keepers faced. In 1846, one of the worst hurricanes ever to strike Key West totally destroyed the lighthouses on Sand Key and Key West. All the people in both lighthouses, six at Sand Key and fourteen at Key West, were killed. A new Key West Lighthouse was completed in 1848. A lightship temporarily replaced the Sand Key Lighthouse until it was rebuilt in 1853. Many people complained about the ineffectiveness of the lightship. Between May 1850 and August 1851, eight ships ran ashore in its vicinity.

At the beginning of the Civil War, secessionists attacked the Cape Florida Lighthouse and smashed the light's lens. The light was not replaced until after the end of the war. Rebel sympathizers also put the Carysfort and Sombrero lights out of operation for a time during the war.

Ship masters and owners, marine insurance agents, and government officials–everyone, in fact, except the wreckers–recognized that the five lights along a treacherous reef extending for two hundred miles–Dry Tortugas, Sand Key, Key West, Carysfort, and Cape Florida–were totally inadequate, even when they were all functioning. Stephen R. Mallory, collector of customs at Key West, said, ". . . although the lights are of the first class, and compare advantageously in brilliancy and reach with any in the world, they are insufficient to afford guides to the mariner . . . let the coast be marked with but half the number of good lights which designate the same extent of our northeastern seaboard, and while the benefits conferred upon our country in a military point of view will be incalculable, the number of shipwrecks on that coast will be reduced to the few that may result from violent hurricanes or other overwhelming calamity." An official of the U.S. Coast Survey said, "If it [the reef] were well lit up as our Northern coast, there would not be so much disaster, and captains running their vessels aground would not have the plea of currents and unaquaintance with the vicinity."

Mallory's remarks notwithstanding, the lights of the lightship *Florida* at Carysfort continued to be the subject of criticism. Some ship masters even went so far as to say they were purposely dimmed or extinguished by keepers in league with the wreckers. But their suspicions were never proved. Lt. David D. Porter, USN, when he was captain of the U.S. mail steamer *Georgia* in 1851, complained that the *Florida*'s lights were "scarcely discernible from the outer ridge of Carysfort Reef at a distance of four to five miles," whereas the lights were rated at twelve miles. The captain of the U.S. mail steamer *Illinois* was equally unhappy with the light at Cape Florida. He remarked that if it were not improved it "had better be dispensed with as the navigator is apt to run ashore looking for it."

As the number of ships wrecked on the reef approached nearly one a week, the cries of ship owners, ship masters, and insurance companies were finally heard in Washington. In 1848, Congress appropriated money to build a lighthouse on Carysfort Reef, where the greatest number of wrecks occurred. It was to be the first of six iron screwpile lighthouses to be built directly on the reef. Lt. George Gordon Meade, who would achieve fame as the Union commander at the battle of Gettysburg, supervised construction of the structure, which was completed in 1852 and still stands today. The other reef lights followed in slow progression: Sand Key (replacing the lightship) in 1853; Sombrero Key, off Key Vaca, in 1858; Alligator Reef, off Lower Matecumbe Key, in 1873; Fowey Rocks, between Cape Florida and Elliott Key, in 1878; and American Shoal, off Sugarloaf Key, in 1880.

The reaction of the wreckers to the lights was predictable. One remarked, "Those damn lights, I wish they was all sunk beneath the sea!" A retired wrecking captain, when asked about the potential usefulness of building a lighthouse on Looe Key, seriously answered that it would not do,

Sombrero Key Lighthouse, off Key Vaca. On several occasions, ship masters mistook lights on the Florida Reef for lights on the Bahama Bank, changed course, and ran aground on the Reef. (courtesy of Monroe County Public Library)

as it would keep all the wrecks off American Shoals.

The lights did not keep all the ships off the reef and, in fact, sometimes led them onto the reef. It is hard to believe, but between 1858 and 1862, at least four ship masters said they mistook the Carysfort light for the Gun Cay light (some forty-five miles distant on the edge of the Bahama Bank), changed course accordingly, and ran aground. Even more difficult to understand is how the master of the British bark *Sir James Ross* mistook the Dry Tortugas light for the Gun Cay light and ended up ashore on French Reef 170 miles later. The more-than-a-little-confused master of the French brig *Jeune Ida* claimed he thought the Sombrero light off Key Vaca was Salt Cay light on Cay Sal Bank (some sixty miles to the south) and went ashore on the reef off Big Pine Key as a result.

Despite their grumbles over the lights, the wreckers in the 1850s had

Alligator Reef Lighthouse, first lighted in 1873. One wrecker said, "I wish those damn lights was sunk below the sea!" (*Harper's New Monthly Magazine*, Vol. XLVIII, March 1874, p. 473. From the collections of The Mariners' Museum, Newport News, Virginia)

more business than ever. An article in *Hunt's Merchants' Magazine* commented: "The increase in the number of beacons, reef signals, buoys, and lighthouses . . . does not seem to lessen the number of accidents to vessels passing through the Florida Straits, but there is no doubt that the average number of accidents to the amount of shipping is less than in former years when the lights and signals did not exist."

Light Keepers Turn Wreckers

A light keeper's primary duty was to keep his light in good working order and burning brightly through the night. No other function was supposed to interfere with maintenance of the light. Yet when a ship went up on the reef nearby, it was impossible for the keepers to ignore it, particularly if no vessel was in sight that could help. The first thing the keepers would do when they saw a wrecked ship was to hoist a distress flag to attract the attention of any passing vessels. If none were in sight, they might row to the nearest harbor to inform a wrecking vessel. And, on some occasions when no wreckers were in the vicinity, they might actively assist in freeing the wrecked vessel.

Upon completing the construction of the Carysfort Lighthouse, Meade instructed the keepers to board all wrecks or vessels in distress and to "succor them as far as it is in [their] power–whether by piloting or the supplying of sustenance or materials of any kind on hand." To enable them to carry out his instructions, he recommended that Carysfort lighthouse be furnished with two oared boats and one sailboat of twelve tons.

The judge of the admiralty court in Key West, however, did not wish to encourage the light keepers to act as wreckers. In 1831, Edward Glover, the light keeper at Dry Tortugas, saw a brig stranded on a nearby reef. There were no vessels in the harbor to go to its aid, so Glover sailed out to the brig in a small boat. The wrecked vessel was the *Concord* from New York on its way to Mobile. She had been through a gale, her sails and rigging were in tatters, and she was in danger of breaking up. The *Concord's* master accepted Glover's offer of assistance and, in accordance with the rules of wrecking, Glover became wreck master. When a fishing sloop, the *Spermaceti,* arrived on the scene, Glover engaged her to assist. The sloop offloaded part of the *Concord's* cargo, took her crew on board, and carried them to Key West. Glover libeled the cargo, valued at $15,000, in the admiralty court. Judge Webb, wishing to discourage light keepers from wrecking, decreed a minimal award of $750 plus expenses.

John Walker, captain of the lightship at Sand Key in 1849, sighted the light of a vessel in distress at half past midnight. Together with four of his crew, he rowed out to the vessel, a schooner, and offered his assistance, which was accepted. Using the schooner's boat, he carried out the schooner's kedge anchor and, when it failed to hold, carried out the bower anchor. In the process of dropping the bower, the boat capsized. While his men clung to the bottom of the capsized boat, Walker swam back to the schooner, got another boat, and rescued them. After towing the schooner's capsized boat to Sand Key and anchoring it, Walker and his men returned to the schooner and assisted in heaving her free. In admiralty court, the master of the schooner maintained that Walker had embellished his story and claimed that it was he and his passengers who actually heaved the schooner afloat. The judge, in keeping with his policy of not making wrecking too attractive for light keepers, awarded the five men from the lightship $50 each.

In 1862, James Oliver and six other men from the Carysfort Lighthouse rowed out to a brig ashore on Elbow Reef and helped her free herself by pumping part of her cargo of molasses overboard. When she was afloat, the lighthouse men rehung the brig's rudder, which enabled her to sail to Key West. For their efforts, the judge awarded the men from Carysfort $60 each.

The head keeper and assistant keeper of the Loggerhead Key Lighthouse hoped to get a handsome reward for saving a bark they sighted flying a distress signal. They sailed a boat out to the bark, some eight miles distant. On boarding, they learned that the captain and two crewmen had died and all the rest of the crewmen were sick except the mate. The lighthouse men helped the mate make sail and piloted the bark into Tortugas harbor. They filed a claim for $800, but the underwriters refused to pay it. Then they libeled the bark in admiralty court. The judge gave a somewhat-less-than-handsome award of $75 for the head keeper and $25 for his assistant.

Surveyors in the Keys—Wreckers Object

Until a few years before the start of the Civil War, the best chart available for navigating the Straits of Florida was one produced eighty years earlier by British cartographer George Gauld. Gauld surveyed the Keys and the reef from 1773 to 1775 but never finished because of the outbreak of the American Revolution. He began surveying at the Dry Tortugas and, working his way to the east, had reached the upper Keys by 1775. As he set out to resume work that year, he said, "We shall begin where we left off last year the Survey to the Eastward towards the Cape [Cape Florida]. It is very laborious and troublesome work among the Kays and Shoals, but as a thorough Knowledge of them is essential for the navigation through the Gulf of Florida [Straits of Florida], the utmost care shall be taken to do them justice."

Considering the facilities and instruments Gauld had available, he did his survey work more than justice. Of his work, Lt. C. R. P. Rodgers, USN, while on coast survey work in 1848, had this to say: "I found the charts of the peninsula [Florida] very inaccurate, with the single exception of Gauld's chart of the Florida Reef, published in 1790, which was evidently a work of merit, and is still valuable, although important changes have taken place since its publication."

An 1847 report to the U.S. Senate on vessels in distress at Key West read in part: "It is not a little surprising that in the *27* years Florida has been held by the U.S., no complete nautical survey has been made of the *Florida Reef*. . . . The charts used by our navigators are the old Spanish charts, and those made by the British from 1763 to 1784 . . . all imperfect in many particulars and erroneous in others. *We have no original American chart of all the reefs and the keys*!"

A U.S. coast survey team went to work to remedy this situation in January 1849, and although preliminary charts were issued, their work was not completed until the beginning of the Civil War. The leader of the survey team was Assistant of the Coast Survey Francis H. Gerdes. Gerdes was a hard-working, meticulous individual who had little regard for the wreckers of the Florida Keys. When he arrived in Key West in January, he wrote,

U.S. Survey Schooner *Gerdes* (*Gerdes Journal,* Sect. VI, Reconnaissance, 1849, courtesy of the National Archives)

"Well, here I am among the wreckers and pirates of Key West–if I can join these islands into a triangulation, it will be a fine thing–so far I have had no difficulties except the bad navigation and constant gales."

After a preliminary reconnaissance of all the Keys, Gerdes began the detailed work of triangulation. This involved establishing several base lines of known length and using beacons planted on the Keys and along the reef to set up a chain of connected triangles. By measuring the angles precisely and knowing the length of the base lines, the positions of the beacons relative to each other could by determined accurately.

The beacons on the reef consisted of iron screwpiles sunk into the coral with mangrove poles thirty to forty feet in height inserted in them. A barrel was fastened to the top of each pole to make it more visible. The survey teams placed the beacons at the most dangerous portions of the reef so they would not only serve as triangulation points, but also as warnings of shoal water to navigators. The beacons could be seen easily with the naked eye from a distance of two to three miles and with a spyglass from six to ten miles. In 1855, the wood poles were replaced with permanent iron poles thirty-six feet in height, each having a vane and an iron cylinder on top. There were fourteen such beacons, each designated by a letter of the alphabet showing in the vane.

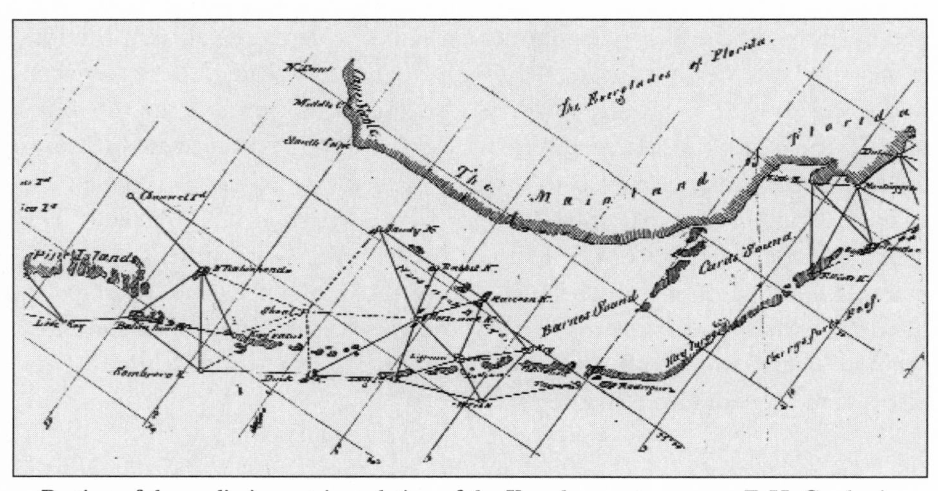

Portion of the preliminary triangulation of the Keys by coast surveyor F. H. Gerdes in 1849 (courtesy of the National Archives)

The beacons received a less-than-enthusiastic reception from the wrecking community. Gerdes wrote in his journal, "It is said openly in Key West that more than five shipwrecks, but certainly that number, were prevented by the timely sight of these beacons. My pilot, Captain Sawyer, a very respectable citizen of Key West [and a wrecker himself] was informed so personally by the Captain of the Wreckers, who mentioned chiefly the signal at Sombrero as destructive of their business." On another occasion, Sawyer informed Gerdes that the wreckers on Key Vaca "had grumbled very much about the tripod [a larger type beacon] on Sombrero [Key], and positively asserted that the beacon alone had prevented four or five vessels from going ashore there."

The wreckers really had no cause to grumble. Even as the beacons and additional lighthouses were being erected and more accurate charts were becoming available, the number of wrecks remained nearly the same or slightly greater. One explanation for this was the increase in traffic through the Straits. But another reason was offered by Capt. James Glynn, USN, commanding the USS *Pensacola.* During a stopover at Key West in January 1860, he had a conversation with Judge Marvin about the wrecking industry. The judge told Glynn that he had good reason to believe there was "a great deal of wrecking by design." This belief was further supported by another conversation Glynn had with the captain of a cotton ship that had gone ashore on the reef two months earlier. The captain said that the loss of his ship was not a thing to be greatly regretted because there were too many ships in the freighting business and shipyards were hurting for business. The captain did not seem to consider it was so great a crime to strand his ship intentionally or even to connive with the wreckers to share in the salvage award. After this conversation, Glynn wrote in his journal: "The recent accurate surveys of the Florida Reefs by the Government of the U. States are not thought to diminish the number of wrecks as was apprehended at first, and, if the majority of the wrecks are intentional, the most accurate charts would only increase the number by shewing [sic] the rogues just where they should make for shore."

Chapter 10

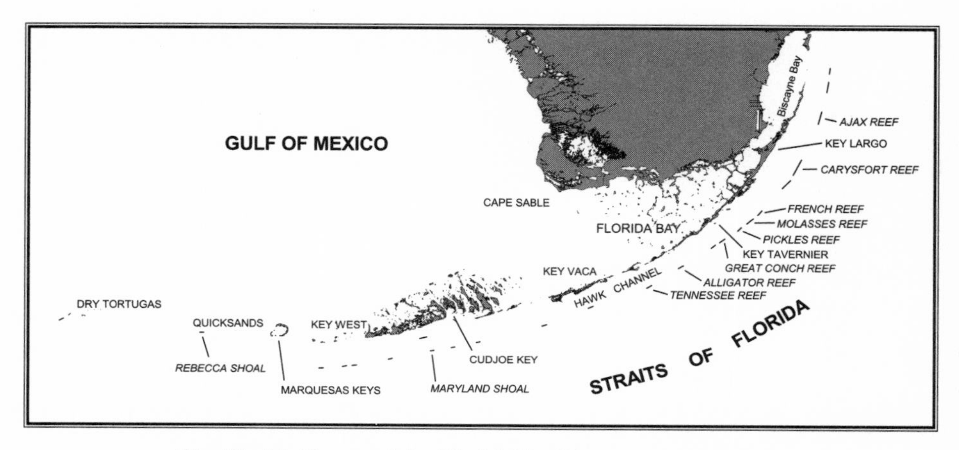

The Florida Keys and the Florida Reef (drawing by Erich Mueller)

THE TWILIGHT YEARS OF THE SAILING WRECKERS

The Civil War and the Blockade

In the middle of the night of January 13, 1861, a column of men with guns on their shoulders stole quietly through the streets of Key West. They were the forty-four members of the U.S. Army's First Artillery Company, making their way from their barracks on the northeastern side of the island to Fort Taylor on the southwestern shore. Florida had seceded from the Union three days earlier, and their commanding officer, Captain James M. Brannan, had waited in vain for guidance from Washington as to whether or not he should man the fort to hold it against possible seizure by secessionists. Urged to secure the fort by the army captain in charge of construction, and knowing that most of the citizens of Key West were pro-South, he decided to take possession of the fort before it was too late. His decision meant that Key West would remain in Union hands, the only Southern port to do so.

Possession of the port of Key West was of enormous strategic value to the North. Immediately after the rebels in Charleston fired on Fort Sumter, President Lincoln declared a blockade of all Southern ports. Key West became the headquarters of the Gulf Blockading Squadron and later, when that command was divided, of the East Gulf Blockading Squadron. Ships of the squadron, which averaged thirty-two in number, were responsible for patrolling the waters from St. Andrews Bay (Panama City) on the Gulf coast to Indian River on the Atlantic coast. During the war, the squadron captured and brought into Key West 199 suspected blockade runners. As an example of the squadron's effectiveness, during a two-month period, its ships captured forty-five out of fifty-two vessels attempting to run the blockade from Havana.

Once the blockade was established, the senior naval officer at Key West issued the following order, "No vessels or boats belonging to this place will be permitted to leave this harbor except those whose owners and crews shall have first taken the oath of allegiance to the U.S. Government." All vessels leaving the harbor were required to show their clearance papers to a guard schooner anchored in the harbor, and no vessels could enter or depart between sunset and sunrise.

As might be expected, with all Gulf ports of the South blockaded, the wrecking business fell into a steep decline. During the four years of the war,

Fort Taylor on the eve of the Civil War, 1861 (*Harper's Weekly*, March 2, 1861, courtesy of Monroe County Public Library)

only twenty salvage cases were heard in the admiralty court at Key West. But because the disposition of the 199 captured vessels also had to be decided, the court docket remained full.

Judge Marvin was known to be sympathetic to the Southern cause and, when hostilities began, announced his intention to resign. But the federal authorities at Key West were unwilling to part with his experience and knowledge in admiralty matters and persuaded him to stay on the bench.

Few of the names of wrecking captains and wrecking vessels prominent before the war appear in the wrecking court records after the war began. Depending on their sympathies, it is probable they joined the Union Navy or the Confederate Navy or became blockade runners.

The majority of the twenty salvage cases decided in admiralty court during the war concerned wrecks of foreign-flag vessels, mostly British, carrying sugar, molasses, rum, cigars, and lumber from Cuban, Mexican, and Jamaican ports. Most of the American vessels that went ashore were transporting soldiers, horses, quartermaster stores, and coal for Union forces. Among the latter was the clipper ship *Stephen R. Mallory,* built in Key West in 1856. The *Mallory* went aground in the Dry Tortugas while carrying troops. After wreckers removed 330 soldiers, the *Mallory's* crew was able to heave her afloat.

Many of the vessels involved in salvaging wrecks during the war were small fishing and sponging craft. Because there were few full-time wrecking vessels patrolling the reef, most of the wrecks were discovered through chance sightings by passing vessels, by lighthouse keepers, or by persons on shore.

Postwar Growth of Key West and Its Seaport

While the wrecking business slowly declined in the decades after the end of the war, two other industries, sponging and cigar making, experienced rapid growth and made Key West the most populous and prosperous city in Florida. Harvesting of sponges had begun in 1849, and, by 1900, there were more than three hundred vessels and two thousand men engaged in the business. Cigar making had its start in 1831. Two years after the end of the Civil War, the fledgling industry was given a boost by the construction of a large cigar-making factory. By 1876, there were twenty-nine factories employing twenty-one hundred workers, many of them refugees from the Ten Years War for Cuban independence.

With the end of the Civil War and the blockade, commercial traffic through the Straits of Florida increased, and many of the ships stopped at Key West to get supplies, water, and repairs, as well as to discharge and embark passengers. In 1873, Mallory Lines steamships began running between New York, Key West, and Galveston on a weekly basis. Two years later, Key West was being served by steamships from Baltimore, Charleston, Havana, and New Orleans. Steamship service between Tampa, Key West, and Havana began in 1887 and between Miami and Key West in 1896. By this time, coastal traffic passing through the port numbered about twenty vessels per month, while foreign traffic passing through customs numbered about twenty-three vessels per month. These figures do not include hundreds of small craft that did not have to enter or clear port.

Shore facilities for shipping, including docks, chandleries, marine railways, sail lofts, and coal-loading piers, were added or improved and enlarged. A new U.S. Customs House, completed in 1891, was the architectural wonder of Key West. In addition to the customs offices, it housed the U.S. District Court for the Southern District of Florida, otherwise

Key West harbor, waterfront, and city view, 1884 (courtesy of Monroe County Public Library)

known as the "wrecking court."

By 1880, sponging, fishing, and freight-carrying vessels operating out of Key West numbered about 450 craft. In November of that same year, the *Key West Democrat* reported that "Mr. Wm. Curry's [leading merchant] wharves have been crowded with shipping. Schooners from New York were unloading their cargoes of dry goods and groceries, boats from Pensacola with lumber, from the Bahamas with fruit, and from Punta Rassa with cattle."

Decline in Shipwrecks

As might be expected, with the opening of Gulf ports after the end of the war, there was an increase in traffic through the Straits and a consequent increase in the number of ships running ashore on the reef. Nevertheless, there were only half as many shipwrecks as before the war, and their numbers soon began to decline even further. By the beginning of the twentieth century, wrecking court cases had fallen from an average of twelve per year immediately following the end of the Civil War to just three per year from 1900 to 1910.

Many factors contributed to the decline in shipwrecks. Three additional lighthouses had been constructed on the reef between 1873 and 1880, accurate charts had become available, and more and more vessels were steam propelled. New railroads carrying freight between the Gulf coast and the east coast of the United States reduced shipping traffic and, consequently, wrecks, particularly those of cotton-carrying ships. For the wreckers, the cotton ships were the most lucrative of all types of shipwrecks. Whereas in the ten-year period immediately following the end of the war, seventeen cotton ships ran up on the reef, in the next ten years, only eight went ashore, and in the ten years after that, only four. Between 1900 and 1910, the wreckers found only two cotton ships on the reef.

Postwar Vessels and Crews

Typical postwar sailing-wrecking vessels and crews were much the same as their prewar predecessors except the vessels were smaller and nearly all were schooner-rigged. The average tonnage of the thirty-nine most successful wrecking vessels in the period between the end of the Civil War and the completion of the Overseas Railroad in 1912 was twenty-seven tons. Only one was more than fifty tons, and none were more than one hundred tons. The most successful wrecking vessel was the schooner *Rapid,* which took part in at least forty-nine salvage operations between 1865 and 1904. The *Rapid* displaced thirteen tons and was described as having "two masts, round stern, scroll figurehead, a centerboard, and was forty-five feet long, fifteen feet wide, and four feet deep."

The names of 312 sailing vessels weighing ten tons or more, each of which salvaged one or more wrecks, appear in the wrecking court records between 1865 and 1911. Most of these were sponge vessels, fishing smacks, freight carriers, and pilot boats for which wrecking was a secondary occupation. There were also many sailing craft with wrecking licenses and boats that would join in salvage operations when the opportunity arose. Many of these were owned by settlers and plantation owners along the Keys. The *Island Home,* for example, a sixty-ton, fifty-nine-foot, inter-keys mail-freight-passenger carrier, built on Plantation Key in 1903, had a wrecking license and participated in five salvage operations between 1904 and 1911.

The schooner *Island Home* salvaged five wrecks between 1904 and 1911.
(courtesy of Monroe County Public Library)

Evidence that a large number of sailing craft were operating in Keys waters in the late 1800s and early 1900s is found in the story of the wreck of a steamship on Alligator Reef in 1904. The wreck was sighted early in the morning, and by noon there were forty-eight sailing craft standing by to render assistance.

Small boats with two- or three-man crews were often allowed to participate in salvage operations to provide the extra manpower needed to offload cargo, man the pumps, or heave around on capstans. Fifteen small boats were among the sixty-seven vessels that worked to salvage cotton bales and staves (barrel wood) from the ship *Northampton,* ashore on Molasses Reef in 1883. Three of the boats carried men and logs to Key Tavernier, where they built piers for landing cotton bales temporarily. During the thirty-four days of salvage operations, these boats supplied the crews of the wrecking vessels with fresh fish and stove wood.

When manpower was short, wrecking captains would sometimes hire men from settlements along the Keys to help with handling cargo. When Cornelius Pinder, captain of the six-ton schooner *Daisy,* with a crew of five men, discovered a British steamship aground on Tennessee Reef in 1881, he knew he could use all the help he could get. In addition to ten other

The schooner *Centennial,* a seventeen-ton, forty-four-foot freight carrier, sponger, and fisherman built in Key West in 1876, salvaged fifteen wrecks between 1876 and 1909. (courtesy of Monroe County Public Library)

schooners that arrived on the scene, he accepted assistance from ten boats and five men from shore. To help unload the Austrian ship *Slobodna,* ashore on Molasses Reef in 1887 with 4,500 bales of cotton, the wreck master employed forty-four men and four boys from shore.

Sailing wreckers continued to use much the same equipment and methods as they did before the war. They hired steam pumps more often, and a centrifugal pump was used in a salvage operation in 1894. Although hardhat diving suits were in common use elsewhere at the time, Keys divers continued to free dive to recover cargo from submerged hulls. The use of "submarine armor" is mentioned in only four wrecking court cases. These took place between 1892 and 1906.

Postwar Captains

For most captains, wrecking in the postwar period was a part-time, as-the-opportunity-arose occupation. This is illustrated by the fact that only twenty percent of the 876 captains whose names appear in wrecking court cases between 1865 and 1911 were ever involved in more than one or two salvage operations. In that forty-six-year period, only nine captains salvaged more than twenty wrecks, and only two captains salvaged more than thirty. While these figures do not include salvage claims settled out of court, they nevertheless make the point that very few captains were able to make wrecking a primary occupation.

Benjamin Baker, known as "Old Ben," was the acknowledged "king of the wreckers" and also the first man to raise pineapples commercially in the Keys. Originally from the Bahamas, unable to read or write, he was described as "tall, shrill-voiced, and hawk-eyed." When he was not cruising the reef looking for wrecks, he divided his time between his two-story home on Key West and his pineapple plantation on Key Largo. He owned at least five schooners, which were used for transporting pineapples as well as for salvaging wrecks. His favorite was the thirteen-ton schooner *Rapid,* which has already been described. In that schooner, he took part in at least seventeen salvage operations, nine of them as wreck master. When he was otherwise occupied, one of his six sons would take command of the schooner.

Capt. Graham J. Lester, wrecking captain, was also master of the Key West–built clipper ship *Stephen R. Mallory* from 1856 to 1863. Between 1867 and 1879, he commanded three pilot-wrecking schooners and salvaged at least seventeen wrecks. (courtesy of Monroe County Public Library)

Wrecking court records show that Baker salvaged at least forty-one wrecks between 1862 and 1880 and was wreck master fifteen times. It is most likely that he salvaged other wrecks that were settled out of court. Baker's closest competitor in the postwar period was Thomas Russell, whose wrecking court record shows thirty-seven salvages but over a much longer period of time, from 1858 to 1901. Russell was wreck master only three times.

Part of Baker's success was due to his location on Key Largo. Aided by his "hawk eyes," he had a view of the most dangerous part of the reef. All but three of his salvages took place off the upper Keys. On three occasions, he sighted wrecks from his house on Key Largo and was the first to arrive on the scene. Once, while out in his pineapple fields, he sighted a wreck and, again, was the first to present his wrecking license to the master.

One of the wrecks he sighted from his house was the ship *Caroline Nesmith,* which had been driven up on the reef two miles from Carysfort Lighthouse by a hurricane in October 1865. The same storm had torn the *Rapid* from her mooring and washed her ashore. Working feverishly through the rest of the day and the night, Baker and his crew of nine got *Rapid* afloat the next morning. At noon, Baker anchored his schooner near the wreck, rowed over, and boarded her. The master of the *Nesmith* informed Baker that he was loaded with twenty-five hundred bales of cotton and that his ship was bilged. Without hesitation, he accepted Baker's offer of assistance. *Rapid's* crew rigged a derrick and began breaking out and hoisting the cotton bales out of the hold. They continued working until eleven o'clock at night, when, totally exhausted, they got some sleep. The next morning, Baker brought the *Rapid* alongside the *Nesmith,* loaded her with twenty-five bales, and carried them into shore. The following day, the *Rapid's* crew took aboard seventeen bales plus the captain, mate, and some of the crew of the *Nesmith* and sailed for Key West, leaving Baker behind to supervise the salvage operations.

Over the next few days, five more schooners arrived on the scene, and Baker took them into a consortship. For a period of three weeks, sixty-two men from the consortship worked unceasingly, breaking out bales and loading them aboard their wrecking vessels. Divers had to swim into the flooded holds to fasten lines to bales, and some of them became temporarily blinded by the foul water. Finally, after twenty-two days of unremitting toil, the wreckers were totally exhausted and Baker decided to abandon any further efforts to retrieve the few remaining bales. During that period, the steamer *Governor Marvin* arrived on the scene and, over Baker's objections, broke out and carried away 250 bales. Two other schooners and two boats from shore salvaged more bales after the original consort had departed. The judge of the district court decreed a salvage award of $60,502, most of which went to Baker's consortship. This was the largest salvage award in the postwar period.

In 1873, Baker anticipated an especially large crop of pineapples and purchased a much larger schooner, the seventy-eight-ton *Whisper,* to carry them to market. With the several schooners he owned, he formed the Baker Wrecking Company. He turned over command of *Rapid* to his son Samuel but did not give up going to sea or wrecking. In between pineapple runs over a period of four years, he steered *Whisper* out to ten wrecks, arriving first twice.

Baker's last salvage operation for which there is a record took place in May 1880, when he was sixty-two years old. Once again, hawk-eyed Old Ben sighted a vessel ashore on the reef, rushed aboard *Rapid,* and was the first to board the wreck. Although a heavy sea rolled the bark over on her side and spoiled most of her cargo of sugar, it was a fitting conclusion to the long career of the "king of wreckers."

Postwar Salvage Operations

As the number of wrecks decreased, so did the number of full-time wrecking vessels. Fewer and fewer vessels went on extended cruises solely for the purpose of discovering wrecks. However, after a storm, some of the larger schooners would get under way "to sight the reef" in hopes of finding a vessel in distress.

As before the Civil War, the greatest number of shipwrecks took place along the reef off the upper Keys. French, Pickles, and Conch Reefs gar-

The brig *Sea Lark* was a total loss off Big Pine Key in 1865. Two wrecking schooners salvaged a thirty-foot boiler and towed it to Key West. (from the collections of The Mariners' Museum Newport News, Virginia)

nered the most wrecks. The next highest incidence of shipwrecks was in the Dry Tortugas area, followed closely by the Marquesas-Quicksands area.

With many spongers, fishermen, and other small craft operating in Keys waters, more and more shipwrecks were discovered by chance than by design. In nearly a third of the salvage operations, wreckers got first word of the shipwreck while lying in port. As the Keys outside of Key West became more populated, first reports of wrecks often came from settlers on shore.

In general, the sailing wreckers conducted salvage operations in much the same way as they did before the war. Because the vessels were smaller and more numerous, the number of vessels involved in a single wreck were often much greater than in prewar years. For example, in 1894, the British steamship *Oxford,* loaded with thirty thousand boxes of sugar, ran aground on Molasses Reef. In all, seventy schooners, nine sloops, and five small boats participated in offloading the sugar before she was pulled off by tugs. In 1901, sixty-three schooners, four sloops, and nine small boats offloaded cotton bales from the Austrian steamship *Styria* after she went aground on French Reef.

One characteristic of Keys wreckers, perseverance, remained unchanged.

Schooners and sloops anchored in Key West harbor around 1900.
All carried wrecking licenses. (courtesy of Florida State Archives)

In nearly every salvage operation, despite physical obstacles, bad weather, foul water, damage to their vessels, or fatigue, most wreckers would not give up until they had heaved the ship off the reef or salvaged the last bale of cotton.

In a consort with six other schooners, Gideon Lowe, captain of the schooner *Arietas,* directed the salvage of the one-thousand-ton steamship *General Meade,* ashore on Maryland Shoals in August 1868. Heavy swells pounded the ship on the bottom and broke off her rudder. After the ship was partially offloaded and heaved afloat, Lowe volunteered to rehang the rudder. Making twenty-five dives in all without benefit of any apparatus, Lowe maneuvered the rudder into position, refastened the rudder chains to the tiller, and freed a hawser that had wrapped itself around the propellor.

The night of April 22, 1879, had been a stormy one. As dawn broke, Benjamin Lowe looked out toward the reef from his home on Key Largo and saw a ship ashore on French Reef. In the face of gale-force winds, he got his nineteen-ton schooner *Casta Diva* under way and beat out to the wreck. On boarding, he learned that she was the American ship *Mary E. Riggs,* loaded with 4,944 bales of cotton. The ship was rolling heavily and striking on the bottom. Lowe could see the deck flexing from the force of the blows and feared the ship would soon go to pieces. But it was too rough to bring a wrecking vessel alongside or to carry out an anchor with a boat. Despite continuous pumping by the ship's crewmen, the water level in the hold rose steadily.

At three o'clock in the morning of the third day after the ship went aground, the weather moderated and Lowe signaled to the six schooners standing by to go to work. At ten in the morning, the wrecking crews boarded, and twelve of them relieved the ship's crewmen at the pumps. The schooner *Rapid,* with Benjamin Baker's son Samuel in charge, was the first alongside, but a squall struck and she broke away. With the seas now making a complete breach over the ship and pounding her on the bottom even harder, she bilged.

On the fifth day, the weather moderated sufficiently to allow the schooner *Marion Mayfield* to get alongside and take on bales of cotton. Other wrecking vessels followed in succession until five o'clock in the evening, when the wind and seas again increased. The pounding broke the ship's bilge timbers and upper deck beams and at midnight forced the salvors to

The steamship *City of Houston,* driven ashore at Saddle Hill Key by a hurricane in October 1876. Grounded in seven feet of water, drawing fourteen feet. Captain of salvage steamer *Cora,* 150-tons, was wreck master. Twenty-seven sailing vessels offloaded cargo for seven days. *Cora* towed her off. (from collections of The Mariners' Museum, Newport News, Virginia)

return to their vessels. In the meantime, Lowe had accepted the services of twenty-one more wrecking vessels that had arrived at the scene.

On the morning of the sixth day, with the weather again moderating, the wreckers reboarded the ship. She now had a heavy list and her deck was broken in on the port side. After they had taken off the ship's crewmen and their baggage, another squall forced the wreckers to return to their vessels. An hour later, they were back aboard and opening the cargo hold hatches. Despite the ominous sounds of deck beams cracking as the ship worked in the swells, they began hoisting bales out of the holds. The hatchways to the lower holds were underwater, so they ripped up the between-decks planking to gain access. Divers then plunged down into the dark water filled with pulpy masses of loose cotton and fastened lines to the bales. The men strained to hoist the bales, which, saturated with water, now weighed over half a ton.

Offloading continued steadily day and night for the next twenty days. More vessels joined the effort until there was a total of forty-four. In all, they saved 4,292 bales, of which 1,784 were dry and 2,508 wet. Of the latter,

1,642 had been saved by diving. The divers all had severe eye pain, and a number of them were blinded for two to three days. The totally exhausted crews abandoned the wreck after saving the rigging and other valuable materials. But there were still six hundred bales of cotton remaining in the submerged hull.

Two weeks later, five of the original wrecking vessels and one fresh one returned to the site, cleared away wreckage, and dived up another 354 bales. The judge of the admiralty court decreed a salvage award of $49,811, which was divided among thirty-six schooners, one sloop, and seven boats with a total of 410 men and 3 boys.

Another extraordinary salvage effort was performed by the crews of the schooners *Cuba* and *Legal Tender* to save the Italian bark *Giovanni A.* The bark had gone aground on the Quicksands in January 1889 and had been abandoned. John Buckley, captain of *Cuba* and wreck master, later learned that the bark's master had become deranged and died after going aground. The demoralized crew left the bark in the boats and rowed to Rebecca Shoals Lighthouse. In a storm, the boats filled with water, broke loose, and drifted away. After eight days, the men were facing starvation. Four of the crewmen and the lighthouse keeper sailed away in the lighthouse boat and reached Key West safely two days later. The crewmen left on the lighthouse were subsequently rescued.

After boarding the bark, the crews of the two wrecking schooners carried out one of the anchors, jettisoned the remainder of the deck load of lumber that the crew had not thrown over, and began pumping. They set the bark's sails and, after hoisting out and throwing over some of the lumber in the cargo hold, moved the bark astern one hundred feet. The next day, they moved her 120 feet and, with a heavy strain on the anchor line, heaved her afloat. With one of their boats ahead taking soundings, they maneuvered her through the shoals until she grounded again. After two more days of carrying out anchors and moving the bark a little each time, they finally got her into a little deeper water. The *Legal Tender* then took soundings to find the best passage out of the shoals and marked it with buoys. On the sixth day after beginning work, the salvors finally sailed the bark clear of the Quicksands.

In justification of the generous salvage award of $6,000 he had decreed,

The schooner *Clifford N. Carver* ashore on Tennessee Reef in 1913
(courtesy of Florida State Archives)

Judge Locke of the district court said, "The salvors are professional licensed wreckers, spending their entire time on this coast and obtaining but a precarious and, most frequently, an insufficient living by assisting vessels, and [are] therefore entitled to the highest rates which could reasonably be given."

Two other postwar salvage cases illustrate the great risks wreckers were willing to take for often meager rewards. Three Key West wrecking captains received word of a schooner sunk off the Cay Sal Bank in March 1869. On arrival, they found the schooner was completely submerged in forty-eight feet of water. They cut a hole in the stern, which was the nearest portion of the wreck to the surface. Free diving, they swam through the hole, into the cabin, and through the cabin into the hold. In the course of many dives, they brought up forty bales of manilla rope, some lumber, a keg of yellow ochre, a piece of chain, an anchor, and some sails worth, in all, $1,000.

Judge Locke decreed a salvage award of sixty-five percent of the value of the goods, far higher than customary, and remarked, "An extremely meritorious case, [the salvors] saved $1,000 worth of property from a totally sunken vessel at great peril to life. The total value divided between the vessels and men would make the shares of the men less than ordinary day wages for the time expended."

A second salvage operation involving great risk to the wreckers took place in February 1873, when a ship loaded with cotton and on fire in the forward hold came into Key West and went aground about one mile from the harbor. After saving sixty bales from the midships and after hatches, the wreckers were forced to leave the ship because of the fire's heat. The next morning they cut a hole in the side of the forward hull at the waterline, hoping that by flooding the hold, the fire would be extinguished. A steam salvage vessel arrived and sprayed water on the ship, but the fire continued to burn.

With spray from the fire pumps soaking them, spars and rigging falling to the deck around them, and the heat of the fire scorching them, wreckers went back aboard and tore up decking to gain access to the lower holds. Before they would go down, the divers demanded an extra award of twenty-five cents for each bale they recovered. Alternately roasting from the heat of the fire and freezing from the cold water in the hold, many of the divers contracted fevers. Others suffered sore eyes and temporary blindness as a result of the tobacco cargo mixed in the water.

The wreckers worked for fifteen days and saved seventeen hundred bales of cotton. The judge decreed a salvage award of $26,837, a tidy sum, but not so much after it was divided among 25 vessels and 230 men.

Postwar Wrongdoing

Among the 258 postwar (up to 1912) wrecking court cases, there are only 4 in which theft of salvaged goods was reported and punished by forfeiture of shares or loss of wrecking licenses. One of those cases stands out above all the rest. In August 1871, the steamship *Mississippi* went ashore forty miles north of Cape Florida. Despite the efforts of fourteen wrecking vessels, she became a total loss. In his response to the wreckers' libel in admiralty court, the *Mississippi's* master claimed that a number of items from the cargo and furnishings of the steamship were missing and that some of them had been found concealed on Loggerhead Key (off Cudjoe Key). As a result of an investigation into the thefts, the captain of the wrecking schooner *Sea Gull* lost his license. His name and the names of seventeen other wrecking crewmen were placed on a "Blacklist" of men "to Whom no Wrecking License will be issued."

Also appearing in the postwar wrecking court records are two cases of serious fraud by wrecking captains. In both cases, insurance company agents uncovered the dishonest acts.

A consort of seven wrecking vessels with Lewis Pierce, captain of the schooner *Three Brothers,* as wreck master heaved the steamer *General Meade* off the reef in September 1866. Before beginning work, Pierce had made an agreement with the steamer's master to get his ship afloat for $25,000. The insurance company's agent discovered that the *General Meade's* master had accepted a kickback of $10,000 when the money was paid at New Orleans sometime later. As a result, Pierce and one other wrecking captain, John Weatherford, lost their licenses and their names were added to the Blacklist.

John H. Geiger Jr., son of wrecking captain John Geiger of prewar fame, libeled the steamship *William Taber* in the wrecking court in April 1867. Geiger claimed that after leaving Key West, the steamship had sprung a leak and then run aground. In his pilot schooner *Richard B. Locke,* Geiger was the first to board. He took the *Taber's* master to Key West to consult with the insurance agent and to procure a steam pump. After returning the master to his ship with the pump, Geiger and a consort of nine wrecking vessels offloaded cargo and got the *Taber* afloat.

In court, the insurance agent charged that the master and chief engineer, in collusion with Geiger, had conspired to sink the steamship. He further claimed that the master and chief engineer tried to bribe the steam pump operator not to pump efficiently. After the ship was moored in Key West, the insurance agent said, he found that the seacocks were open and the ship was filling with water. Apparently, the agent's charges were substantiated. Geiger lost his license and his name was added to the Blacklist.

Considering that there were only two known serious violations of ethics by wrecking captains over a period of forty-six years, it is reasonable to conclude that the vast majority of captains were honest men.

The Age of Sailing Wrecking Vessels Draws to a Close

Steam-powered salvage vessels began to appear in wrecking court records in the 1870s. In that decade, fourteen percent of the court-adjudicated salvage cases included one or more steam-powered salvage vessels. By the first decade of the 1900s, steamers and tugs were engaged in slightly over half of all salvage cases heard in admiralty court.

The steam salvage vessels usually worked with a group of sailing-wrecking vessels. After the sailing wreckers had offloaded cargo, the principal functions of the steam vessels were to tug the wreck off the reef and tow it back to Key West. Because the steam vessels had greater capabilities than the sailing vessels and cost more to operate, the admiralty court judge, as a rule, awarded them higher rates of salvage.

Around the 1890s, two local salvage companies with steam-powered vessels appeared on the scene. They were the Key West Wrecking Company and the Key West Salvage and Towage Company. Around 1900, the New York salvage company Merritt and Chapman established an agency in Key West, and, in 1907, one of their tugs assisted in saving a steamship aground in the Marquesas.

One of the leading wrecking captains of the late 1800s and early 1900s was Bradish Johnson. His career illustrated the shift in salvage operations from sail to steam and from manpower to machine power.

A graduate of the U.S. Naval Academy from a well-to-do family, Johnson left the Navy to find an even more adventurous life at sea. In a schooner owned in partnership with his brother, Johnson illegally hunted seals and sea otters in the Bering Sea, ran guns to revolutionaries in Mexico, and narrowly escaped execution after being captured.

Coming to Key West in 1882 to assist in building a pier for the Navy, his adventurous spirit attracted him to the wrecking business, and he decided to stay. He married Irene Bethel, a local Bahamian girl, and, after a little experience on wrecking vessels, built his own thirty-five-ton, fifty-one-foot schooner, which he named *Irene.* In one of his first salvage operations with *Irene,* he took over salvage of a sunken schooner that the regular wrecking

Bradish "Hog" Johnson, a prominent wrecking captain in the late 1800s and early 1900s, led the transition from sail to steam wrecking vessels.
(courtesy of Florida State Archives)

vessels had abandoned. Together with the crew of another schooner, he pumped her out, repaired a large hole in her underwater hull, heaved her off the reef, rerigged her, and sailed her to Key West.

This early salvage operation was typical of Johnson's determination, ingenuity, and skill. Tall and handsome, with a powerful build and a daredevil attitude, Johnson outwitted his competitors in so many salvage operations that he acquired the nickname "Hog." He was also an expert hard-hat diver. When he learned from an insurance agent in Key West that a steamer was ashore on Grand Bahama Bank, he persuaded a revenue cutter to tow his schooner across the Straits to the site. The steamer was bilged, full of water, and in a foreign country's waters. None of this deterred Johnson. In his hard-hat diving suit, Johnson inspected the ship's bottom and repaired part of the damage but was unable to repair a large hole. He then proceeded to dive into the cargo hold and, working in water fouled by potash, in three days saved $17,000 worth of cargo.

Diver going over the side to inspect wrecked ship's hull. Bradish Johnson was an accomplished hard-hat diver.
(*Harper's Weekly*, July 3, 1880. From the collections of The Mariners' Museum, Newport News, Virginia)

Johnson shifted from sail to steam in 1893, taking command of the wrecking tug *O. C. Williams*. In 1901, he became master of the wrecking tug *George W. Childs,* owned by the Key West Salvage and Towage Company. Sometime in this period, he joined three other men in forming the Key West Wrecking Company, which, according to one source, took the cream of the wrecking business crop for the next fifteen years.

When he wasn't involved in salvage work, Johnson engaged in other adventurous enterprises, such as secretly supplying coal to the filibustering tug *Three Friends*, which was running arms to the revolution in Cuba illegally. He also sailed a small open boat across the Straits of Florida from Nassau to Key West.

One of the last lucrative salvage jobs for the Keys sailing wreckers was the Spanish steamer *Alicia,* which went ashore on Ajax Reef in April 1905 and bilged. She was loaded with a large cargo of valuable

Wrecking schooners salvaging the wreck of the steamer *Alicia*, ashore on Ajax Reef in 1905 and one of the last "rich" hauls for the sailing wreckers (courtesy of Monroe County Public Library)

merchandise–including fine silks, linens, household furniture, pianos, wines, and liquors–being imported to Havana from Europe. Arthur Lowe, in his little ten-ton schooner, *Mount Olive,* was the first to board her. He made an agreement with the master to get the steamer off for $5,000, but, when it was found that she was bilged, the agreement was canceled.

In a matter of hours, a huge fleet of mostly small sailing craft surrounded the wreck, all eager for a share in the spoils. In all, there were forty-seven schooners, seven sloops, twenty-two small boats, and one steam launch. When all the dry cargo had been offloaded, divers entered the flooded cargo holds and, mostly by feel, attached lines to boxes, barrels, and other cargo containers. As the days passed, fermenting rice, rotting codfish, and dissolving potash fouled the water. Some of the divers were blinded for twenty-four hours. After two weeks, the divers refused to work anymore, and the wreck was abandoned. The final salvage award was $17,690, but that had to be divided among the seventy-seven vessels and five hundred men who worked in the operation.

As the years passed, the number of wrecks and the number of sailing vessels involved in salvaging them continued to decline. In 1920, the New York salvage firm Merritt and Chapman bought out the last of the local Keys wreckers, and, one year later, the District Court of the Southern District of Florida closed its register of wrecking licenses. With its closing, an adventurous, often-dangerous, highly competitive, sometimes-lucrative, and often-misunderstood profession passed into history.

Bibliography

Introduction

Hersey, John. *Key West Tales.* New York: Alfred A. Knopf, 1994.

Strabel, Thelma. *Reap the Wild Wind.* New York: Triangle Books, 1942.

Chapter 1

Albury, Paul. *The Story of the Bahamas.* London: Macmillan Education Limited, 1975.

Arnade, Charles W. "Florida Keys: English or Spanish in 1763?" *Tequesta,* No. 15 (1955): 41–53.

The Bahama Gazette and *The Royal Gazette and Bahamian Advertizer.* Various issues from 1784 to 1825 on microfilm at the Monroe County Public Library, Key West.

Carr, Robert S. "Prehistoric Settlement of the Florida Keys." *The Florida Keys Environmental Story.* Dan Gallagher, Ph.D., editor-in-chief. Big Pine Key: Monroe County Environmental Education Advisory Council, Inc., 1997: 68–69.

Charlevoix's Louisiana. Selections from the *History and the Journal* by Pierre F. X. de Charlevoix. Charles E. O'Neill, editor. Baton Rouge: Louisiana State University Press, 1977.

The Collector of Customs (Pensacola) to the Secretary of the Treasury Concerning Bahamian Wreckers on Florida Coast, November 26, 1821. *Territorial Papers of the U.S., The Territory of Florida, Vol. 22, 1821–1824.* Washington, D.C.: U.S. Government Printing Office, 1960: 282.

Craton, Michael. *A History of the Bahamas.* London: Collins, 1962.

Cutler, Carl C. *Mystic, the Story of a Small New England Seaport.* Mystic, Connecticut: Mystic Seaport Museum Inc., 1945.

"Description of Seven Salvage Techniques by Pedro de Ledesma ca. 1623." (Madrid, *Museo Naval, MS. 1035, Seccion C.*) Documentary Sources–1554 Fleet. Texas Antiquities Committee: 316–328.

Documents relating to the loss of the 1733 *flota* from the *Archivo General de Indias: Contratación 5102, 5147. Indiferente General 57, 2021, 2300.* Translated by Jack Haskins. Florida Collection, Monroe County Public Library, Helen Wadley Branch Library, Islamorada, Florida.

Employment of Keys natives as salvage divers on wreck of *Maravillas. Archivo General de Indias, Contraduria 1115.* Notes from verbal translation by Dr. Eugene Lyon.

"Establishing an Underwater Archaeological Preserve in the Florida Keys." Florida Archaeological Reports 7. Edited by Roger C. Smith, Ph.D., 3–15. Prepared by Bureau of Archaeological Research, Division of Historical Resources, Florida Department of State, Tallahassee, 1988.

Fontaneda, Do. d'Escalante. *Memoir of Do. d'Escalante Fontaneda Respecting Florida Written in Spain, About the Year 1575.* Translated by Buckingham Smith. Annotated by David O. True. Coral Gables, Florida: Glades House, 1944.

Gauld, George. *Observations on the Florida Kays, Reef, and Gulf with Directions for Sailing Among the Kays.* London: 1796.

Goggin, John M., and Frank H. Sommer. "Excavations on Upper Matecumbe Key, Florida." *Yale University Publications in Anthropology,* No. 41: 21–28. New Haven: Yale University Press, 1949.

John Du Bose to John Rodman, letter concerning Bahamian wreckers in Keys, May 21, 1823. *The Territorial Papers of the U.S., The Territory of Florida, Vol. 22, 1821–1824.* Washington, D.C.: U.S. Government Printing Office, 1960: 684–685.

Lyon, Eugene. *The Search for the Atocha.* New York: Harper and Row, 1979.

Lyon, Eugene. "The 1622 *Tierra Firme Flota* Salvage and the Florida Keys Natives." An address to the Florida Keys Maritime History Conference at Key West, May 6, 2000.

Marques de Cadereita to the Crown, letter reporting the destruction of the 1622 *flota* and measures taken to locate and recover treasure from the sunken galleons. Havana, January 10, 1623. *Archivo General de Indias, Santo Domingo 132.*

Marx, Robert F. *Shipwrecks in Florida Waters.* Chuluota, Florida: The Mickler House, 1979.

Meylach, Martin. *Diving to a Flash of Gold.* Garden City, New York: Doubleday and Co., 1971.

Peters, Thelma. "The American Loyalists in the Bahama Islands: Who They Were." *Florida Historical Quarterly,* Vol. XXX, No. 3 (June 1962): 235–236.

Potter, John S. Jr. *The Treasure Diver's Guide,* Revised Edition. New York: Bonanza Books, 1972.

Schene, Michael G. "The Early Florida Salvage Industry." *American Neptune,* Vol. 38, No. 4 (October 1978): 262–263.

Vignoles, Charles. *Observations Upon the Floridas.* Facsimile reproduction of 1823 edition. Gainesville: University Presses of Florida, 1977.

Wright, James M. "The Wrecking System of the Bahama Islands." *Political Science Quarterly,* Vol. XXX, No. 4 (1915): 618–644.

Chapter 2

Browne, Jefferson B. *Key West: The Old and the New.* Facsimile reproduction of the 1912 edition. Gainesville: University of Florida Press, 1973.

Diary of William R. Hackley, Key West attorney, 1830–1857. Copy at Monroe County Public Library, Key West.

Fryman, Mildred L. "Historical Study for Proposed Key West Museum." Prepared for Division of Recreation and Parks by the Bureau of Historic Sites and Properties; Division of Archives, History and Records Management; Florida Department of State. Miscellaneous Project Report Series No. 11. Tallahassee: 1974.

Key West Enquirer. Various issues, 1834–1836.

Key West Customs House. Entrances and Clearances, various years, January 1869 to December 1889. Microfilm copy from original ledgers at National Archives. Monroe County Public Library, Key West.

Matthew C. Perry to the Secretary of the Navy, U.S. Schooner *Shark,* March 28, 1822, report of examination of Key West and taking possession. *Territorial Papers of the U.S., The Territory of Florida, Vol. 22, 1821–1824.* Washington, D.C.: U.S. Government Printing Office, 1960: 385–387.

Memorandum by John W. Simonton, December 7, 1821, concerning advantages of Key West for commerce and as a depot for wrecked property. *Territorial Papers of the U.S., The Territory of Florida, Vol. 22, 1821–1824.* Washington, D.C.: U.S. Government Printing Office, 1960: 411.

Memorial of John W. Simonton and others claiming reimbursement for damages done by the antipiracy squadron under Commodore

Porter. House of Representatives, 30th Congress, First Session, Report No. 189, February 9, 1848. Washington, D.C.: U.S. Government Printing Office, 1848.

Thurston, William Nathaniel. "A Study of Maritime Activity in Florida in the Nineteenth Century." Ph.D. thesis, Florida State University, 1972.

Chapter 3

Admiralty Final Record Books, U.S. District Court, Southern District of Florida, Key West, 1829–1911. Microfilm copy at Monroe County Public Library, Key West.

Bearss, Edwin C. "Shipwreck Study–The Dry Tortugas." Washington, D.C. : U.S. Department of the Interior, National Park Service, Eastern Service Center, Office of History and Historic Architecture, 1971.

Browne. *Key West: The Old and the New.*

Diary of William R. Hackley.

Diddle, Albert W. "Adjudication of Shipwrecking Claims at Key West in 1831." *Tequesta* (1946): 44–49.

Dodd, Dorothy. "The Wrecking Business on the Florida Reef." *Florida Historical Quarterly,* Vol. XXII, No. 4 (April 1944): 171–199.

Halas, Judith F., principal investigator. "An Inventory of Shipwrecks, Groundings, and Cultural Marine Resources within the Key Largo National Marine Sanctuary Region: Preliminary Report." NOAA Technical Memorandum NOS MEMD #NA87AA-H-CZ007, Key Largo National Marine Sanctuary, June 1988.

Hammond, E. A., editor. "Wreckers and Wrecking on the Florida Reef, 1829–1832." *Florida Historical Quarterly,* Vol. XLI, No. 3 (Jan. 1963): 239–273.

Hunt, Freeman. "Wrecks, Wrecking, Wreckers, and Wreckees on the Florida Reef." *The Merchants' Magazine and Commercial Review*, Vol. VI (1842): 349–354.

Key West Enquirer. Various issues, 1834–1836.

Letter from John W. Simonton to Philip P. Barbour [U.S. Representative] Wash. City, March 5, 1828. *Territorial Papers of the United States, The Territory of Florida, Vol. XXIII, 1824–1828.* Washington, D.C.: U.S. Government Printing Office, 1960: 1032–1034.

Letter from S. R. Mallory, collector of the port of Key West, to the Superintendent of the Coast Survey, relative to the Florida keys and reefs. Dec. 28, 1848. *Report to the Secretary of the Treasury communicating a report from the Superintendent of the Coast Survey, in relation to the survey of the coast of Florida.* Exec. Doc. No. 30, 30th Cong., 2nd session.
Marvin, William. *A Treatise on the Law of Wreck and Salvage.* Boston: Little, Brown, 1858.
Memorial to Congress by Inhabitants of Key West, December 29, 1826. *Territorial Papers of the U.S., The Territory of Florida, Vol. XXIII, 1824–1828:* Washington, D.C.: U.S. Government Printing Office, 1960: 699–702.
Memorial to Congress by Masters and Owners of Vessels in the Territory, September 13, 1829. *Territorial Papers of the U.S., The Territory of Florida, Vol. XXIV, 1828–1834.* Washington, D.C.: U.S. Government Printing Office, 1960: 265–267.
Scott, Kenneth. "The City of Wreckers–Key West Letters of 1838." *Florida Historical Quarterly,* Vol. XXV, No. 2 (October 1946): 191–201.
Singer, Steven D. *Shipwrecks of Florida,* Second Edition. Sarasota, Florida: Pineapple Press, Inc., 1998.

Chapter 4

Admiralty Final Record Books.
Bearss. "Shipwreck Study–Dry Tortugas."
Browne. *Key West: The Old and the New.*
Diary of William R. Hackley.
Hammond. "Wreckers and Wrecking on the Florida Reef, 1829–1832."
Marvin. *A Treatise on the Law of Wreck and Salvage.*
Shipping news in the following newspapers for the years indicated:
Key West Register and Commercial Advertizer, 1829.
Key West Enquirer, 1834–1836.
Key West Gazette, 1832, 1845.
Key to the Gulf, 1855, 1858–1860.
Singer. *Shipwrecks of Florida.*
Viele, John. "Sailing Craft of the Florida Keys." *Tequesta,* No. LII (1992): 7–19.

Chapter 5

Admiralty Final Record Books.

"1856: A Letter Concerning Indian Key." *History Talk from the Upper Florida Keys,* Issue 4 (Summer 1998): 55.

Browne. *Key West: The Old and the New.*

Census of the United States. Florida: Dade and Monroe Counties, 1850, 1860, 1870, and 1880.

Certificates of Enrollment and Registration for Key West, Florida. Record Group 41, National Archives.

Diary of William R. Hackley.

Dodd, Dorothy. "The Wrecking Business on the Florida Reef."

Genealogical records of Geiger, Bethel, and Roberts families on file at Monroe County Public Library, Key West.

Gerdes, Francis H., assistant, U.S. Coast Survey. "Sec. VI, U.S. Coast and Geodetic Survey, A. D. Bache, Supt.: An Interesting Journal by F. H. Gerdes on Florida Reefs, 1848–9, Reconnaissance in Sec. VI." Record Group 23, National Archives.

Hammond. "Wreckers and Wrecking on the Florida Reef, 1829–1832."

Harllee, William Curry. *Kinfolks–A Genealogical and Biographical Record of Benjamin and Mary Curry, Samuel and Amelia (Russell) Kemp* (1934). Special Edition. Portland, Oregon: Clefan Publishing, 1998.

Key West Enquirer (November 26, 1838): p. 3.

Lytton, Catherine Lowe. "Captain Richard Roberts–Civil War Blockade Runner." *United Daughters of the Confederacy Magazine* (May 1997): 17.

Marvin. *A Treatise on the Law of Wreck and Salvage.*

New York Daily Times (July 7, 1854).

Nordoff, C. "Wrecking on the Florida Keys." *Harper's New Monthly Magazine* (April 1859): 577–586.

"Our Pilot Boats." *Key West Gazette* (Dec. 13, 1845): 3.

Pensacola Gazette (November 2, 1827): 3.

Perrine, Henry. *A True Story of Some Eventful Years in Grandpa's Life.* Buffalo, New York: E. H. Hutchinson, 1885.

"Population and Trade of Key West; the Wrecking Business, &c." Correspondence of the *Charleston Courier,* Key West, Jan. 22, 1854, published in the *New York Daily Times,* July 7, 1854.

Walker, Jonathan. *Trial and Imprisonment of Jonathan Walker, At Pensacola Florida, for Aiding Slaves to Escape from Bondage.* A facsimile reproduction of the 1845 edition. Gainesville: University Presses of Florida, 1974.

Chapter 6

Admiralty Final Record Books.

Bache, Richard Meade. *The Young Wrecker of the Florida Reef or the Trials and Adventures of Fred Ransom.* Philadelphia: Claxton, Remsen, and Haffelfinger, 1870.

Key West Enquirer (Oct. 3, 1835): 3.

Scott. "The City of Wreckers–Key West Letters of 1838."

Chapter 7

25th Congress, 2nd Session, House of Representatives. Report No. 4, Samuel Sanderson, Dec. 14, 1837.

Admiralty Final Record Books.

Buker, George E. "Lieutenant Levin M. Powell USN, Pioneer of Riverine Warfare." *Florida Historical Quarterly,* No. 3 (January 1969): 262.

Hambright, Tom. "Sea Monster on Carysfort Reef." *Florida Keys Sea Heritage Journal,* Vol. 1, No. 3 (Spring 1991): 11.

Koch, Dr. Albert C. *Travel diary of a journey through a part of the United States of North America in the years 1844 to 1846.* Excerpt provided by Missouri Historical Society to the Monroe County Public Library.

Memorial to the Secretary of State by John Morrison and Others. *Territorial Papers of the U.S., The Territory of Florida, Vol. XXIII, 1824–1828.* Washington, D.C.: U.S. Government Printing Office, 1960: 990–992.

Perrine. *A True Story of Some Eventful Years in Grandpa's Life.*

"The ship *Spermo* . . . totally lost on Alligator Reef." *Savannah Georgian* (Feb. 5, 1827): 2

Swanson, Gail. "1827 drama: Slave ship wrecks on Carysfort Reef." Compilation of documents related to the wreck of the Spanish slave ship *Guerrero* on Dec. 20, 1827. Gift to the Monroe County Public Library, Islamorada, Florida, by Gail Swanson, 1992.

Swanson, Gail. "The Africans of the Slave Ship *Guerrero.*" Privately pub-

lished paper for the 200th anniversary of the Kingsley Plantation, October 1998.
"William Adee Whitehead's Reminiscences of Key West." Edited by Thelma Peters. *Tequesta,* No. XXV (1965): 20.

Chapter 8

Admiralty Final Record Books.
"Case in Admiralty. Jacob Houseman vs. Proceeds arising from sale of the Brig *Halcyon*–Oliver O'Hara, Respondent." *Key West Gazette* (May 23, 1832): 1.
"Case in Admiralty, Oliver O'Hara, Ass'ce of Mariatigue, Knight & Co. vs. The Brig *Halcyon,* &c. & Jacob Houseman & John R. Western, Claimants as Salvors." *Key West Gazette* (Nov. 30, 1831): 1.
Davis, T. Frederick. "Pioneer Florida–Indian Key and Wrecking in 1833." *Florida Historical Quarterly,* Vol. XXII, No. 2 (October 1943): 57–61.
Dodd, Dorothy. "Jacob Housman of Indian Key." *Tequesta* , No. 8 (1948): 3–19.
Howe, Charles. "A Letter from Indian Key, 1840." *Florida Historical Quarterly,* Vol. XX, No. 2 (Oct. 1941): 197–202.
Letter from F. A. Browne, Acting Collector, Key West, charging Jacob Housman with robbery in the case of the brig *Revenge* of Sept. 25, 1825, and reply by Jacob Housman, "To The Public," Oct. 29, 1825. From the *New York Gazette* in the *East Florida Herald* (Nov. 8, 1825): 4.
"Libel of Daniel C. Mellus vs. Brig *Vigilant*." *Key West Register and Commercial Advertizer* (April 23, 1829): 3.
"Libel of French Consul vs. salvaged cargo of Brig *Revenge*." *East Florida Herald* (Oct. 4, 1825): 3.
Miller, W. Randy. "The Case of the Brig *Halcyon*: A Study in Old Key West Admiralty Law." *The Journal of Maritime Law and Commerce,* Vol. 27, No. 2 (April 1996): 311–321.
Peters, Thelma. Introduction to *A Sketch of the History of Key West* by Walter C. Maloney. Facsimile reproduction of the 1876 edition. Gainesville: University of Florida Press, 1968
A private Journal kept aboard the USS *Pensacola* on a passage from

Pensacola, Florida, to Norfolk, Virginia, by James Glynn, Captain USN. Entry for Thursday, January 5, 1860. Collections of the Mariners' Museum, Newport News, Virginia.

Remonstrance to Congress by Inhabitants of Monroe County [against Indian Key being made a port of entry, no date, 1836]. *Territorial Papers of the United States, The Territory of Florida, Vol. XXV, 1834–1839.* Washington, D.C.: U.S. Government Printing Office, 1960: 249–253.

Schene, Michael G. "History of Indian Key." Miscellaneous Project Report Series No. 8. Tallahassee: Bureau of Historic Sites and Properties; Division of Archives, History, and Records Management; Florida Department of State, 1973.

Chapter 9

Dean, Love. *Lighthouses of the Florida Keys.* Key West: Historic Florida Keys Foundation, Inc., 1992.

Gerdes. Journal.

Letter from Lieutenant C. R. P. Rodgers, United States Navy, on coast survey service to the superintendent of the coast survey relative to the coast of Florida, Dec. 30, 1848. Letter from S. R. Mallory, collector of the port of Key West, to the Superintendent of the Coast Survey, relative to the Florida Keys and reefs. Dec. 28, 1848. *Report to the Secretary of the Treasury communicating a report from the Superintendent of the Coast Survey, in relation to the survey of the coast of Florida.* Exec. Doc. No. 30, 30th Cong., 2nd session. Feb. 15, 1849.

Maloney, William C. *A Sketch of the History of Key West, Florida.* Facsimile reproduction of the 1876 edition. Gainesville: University of Florida Press, 1968.

Silvia, Diane, and David G. Whall. "Beacons of the Florida Keys as Submerged Cultural Resources." *Underwater Archaeology* (1999): 71–79.

Chapter 10

Admiralty Final Record Books.

Beare, Nikki. *Pirates, Pineapples, and People.* Miami: Atlantic Publishing Co., 1961.

Bibliography

Birse, Shepard. *Lore of the Wreckers*. Boston: Beacon Press, 1961.

"Blacklist to Whom no Wrecking License will be issued with reason of forfeiture." Included in "Register of Wreckers 1860–1920." Monroe County Public Library, Key West.

Gilpin, Vincent. "Bradish W. Johnson, *Master Wrecker*." *Tequesta,* Vol. 1, No. 1(March 1941): 21–32.

Halas. "An Inventory of Shipwrecks, Groundings, and Cultural Marine Resources. . . ."

Ludlum, Stuart, compiler and editor. *Exploring Florida 100 Years Ago*. New York: Brodock & Ludlum Publications, 1973.

Munroe, Ralph M., and Vincent Gilpin. *The Commodore's Story*. Miami: Historical Association of Southern Florida, 1985.

Official Records of the Union and Confederate Navies in the War of the Rebellion. Series 1, Vol. 4, Operations: Gulf of Mexico Nov. 15,1860–Jun. 7. 1861. Atlantic Coast Jan. 1–May 13,1861. Potomac and Rappahanock Rivers Jan. 5–Dec. 7 1861. Washington, D.C.: 1896.

Singer. *Shipwrecks of Florida.*

Treasury Department, U.S. Life Saving Service. "Statement of Maritime Disasters, Vessels In or Near Coast of Florida, June 1, 1869 to June 30, 1879." Washington, July 19, 1879. Record Group 26, National Archives.

Index

Illustrations are indicated in boldface type.